CULTURE SMART!
UAE

Jessica Hill and John Walsh

·K·U·P·E·R·A·R·D·

ISBN 978 1 85733 874 4

British Library Cataloguing in Publication Data
A CIP catalogue entry for this book is available from the British Library

First published in Great Britain
by Kuperard, an imprint of Bravo Ltd
59 Hutton Grove, London N12 8DS
Tel: +44 (0) 20 8446 2440 Fax: +44 (0) 20 8446 2441
www.culturesmart.co.uk
Inquiries: sales@kuperard.co.uk

Series Editor Geoffrey Chesler
Design Bobby Birchall

Printed in India

About the Author

JESSICA HILL is a freelance journalist. A graduate in Contemporary History from the University of Sussex, she went on to complete a NCTJ diploma in newspaper journalism at the University of Brighton. In 2011 she moved to Abu Dhabi where she wrote for the UAE's most popular English newspaper, *The National*. Today she lives in Colchester, UK, and remains a regular contributor to *The National* newspaper, returning to the UAE frequently for assignments.

JOHN WALSH is Assistant Professor in Marketing and Communication at Shinawatra University in Bangkok, Thailand. His doctorate, from the University of Oxford, was for research on international management. He has written extensively for learned journals, contributed to a number of encyclopedias, undertaken media and consultancy work, and also been widely published in non-academic fields. Having lived and worked in Sudan, Greece, South Korea, Australia, and the United Arab Emirates, he now lives in Bangkok.

contents

contents

Map of the UAE

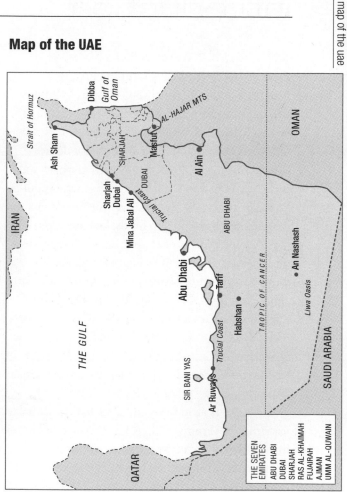

THE SEVEN
EMIRATES
ABU DHABI
DUBAI
SHARJAH
RAS AL-KHAIMAH
FUJAIRAH
AJMAN
UMM AL-QUWAIN

introduction

While the UAE is one of the most conservative
societies in the world, it also prides itself on
being one of the most forward-looking. With its
strikingly modern architecture and showcasing of
new technologies, it can be easy to forget that only
fifty years ago, the UAE was a very poor desert
country, on the peripheries of the Arab world and
Britain's colonial empire. The older generation of
Emiratis, who today preside over their country's
multibillion dollar wealth funds, had to endure a
harsh, nomadic existence, their survival dependent
that the annual rains would fall each winter to
avert famine. The discovery of oil changed all that,
although it took the wise leadership of Sheikh
Zayed bin Sultan al Nahyan (1918–2004) to ensure
that the blessings of wealth did not become a curse.
He left behind a powerful legacy in which desert
tradition is balanced with modernity and tolerance
that continues to this day.

The UAE is ambitious and aims to be a global
leader in the Arab world. An interview conducted
in 2007 by CBS's "60 Minutes" news program
with Sheikh Mohammed bin Rashid al Maktoum,
ruler of Dubai and Prime Minister of the UAE,
demonstrates clearly the goals the country has set
itself. In answer to the question on his homeland,

"What do you want this place to be?" he replied:

"I want it to be number one. Not in the region, but in the world. In everything—higher education, health, and housing. Just making my people have the highest way of living."

Asked why he wanted everything to be the biggest, the tallest, he replied,

"Why not?"

Futuristic in their business endeavors and welcoming of technological breakthroughs in areas of particular interest—artificial intelligence and space travel (the UAE plans to set up a space agency and send the Arab world's first mission to Mars by 2021)—the Emiratis still manage to maintain an enduring bond with the desert, and a tight-knit family structure that is waning in other parts of the developed world. The UAE also manages to retain its Islamic essence, and the daily routine of life is accompanied by the cadences of the muezzin's calls to prayer from the country's many mosques.

Combined with the legendary Arabic sense of hospitality, this makes the UAE a potentially extremely rewarding place to visit. This book will introduce you to the history and culture of the Emiratis, and smooth your path toward full enjoyment of a fascinating experience.

Key Facts

Official Name	United Arab Emirates (Al Imarat al Arabiyah al Muttahidah)	Member of the Gulf Cooperation Council, Organization of Petroleum Exporting Countries
Capital City	Abu Dhabi Pop. of Abu Dhabi Emirate is approx. 2.908 million (1,857,618 Males, 1,050,555 Females)	20 percent of the population of the UAE live in rural areas.
Largest cities	Dubai, Abu Dhabi, Sharjah	
Population	9,487,826	
Ethnic Makeup	The largest group of non-UAE nationals are South Asian (58%), followed by other Asians (17%) and Western expatriates (8.5%). Only 10% of the population are UAE nationals.	The proportions vary according to demand for migrant labor. The UAE also has the highest gender imbalance in the world with a male/female ratio of 2.2, or 2.75 for the 15–65 age group.
Age Structure	0-14: 21% 15-64: 78% 65: 1% 73% of the adult (15+) population is male.	
Area	32,278 sq. miles (83,600 sq. km)	Composed of seven individual Emirates.
Geography	Located on northern coast of Arabian Peninsula along the coast of the Persian Gulf, and bordered by Saudi Arabia and Oman.	
Terrain	Mostly desert, with rolling dunes and generally flat apart from eastern mountains	
Climate	Desert climate, hot and humid on coast	

Natural Resources	Petroleum, natural gas	Less than 4% of land is suitable for agriculture.
Currency	Emirati dirham, which is pegged to the American dollar.	1 Dirham = US $0.272264
Language	Arabic	English is widely understood.
Religion	Islam is the state religion: 76% of the population is Muslim, mostly Sunni, and 16% are Shi'a.	
Government	Federation of Seven Emirates. Powers are divided between Federal and Emirate-level governments.	
Media	All Emirates have at least one state controlled TV station, and several satellite stations offering different packages. Both English- and Arabic-language radio stations are available. The media are controlled to prevent broadcast of inappropriate or indecent material.	National newspapers published in Dubai include the Arabic language *Al Bayan*, *Al Khaleej*, and *Al Ittihad*, as well as English-language papers *The National*, *Gulf News* and *Khaleej Times*.
Electricity	220/240 volts, 50 Hz	Three-prong plugs are used.
DVD/Video	DVD PAL, Region 2	
Internet Domain	.ae	
Telephone	The UAE's country code is 971.	Dialing out: 00 + country code
Time Zone	GMT + 4 hours	No daylight saving time

LAND & PEOPLE

GEOGRAPHY

The UAE is located on the northern part of
the Arabian Peninsula, and lies along the salty
waters of the Arabian Gulf. The land itself is
mostly flat and almost entirely desert in the
interior. To the east, the border with Oman is
marked by the Al Hajar Mountains, which rise
to a maximum of around 6,500 feet (1981 m),
while to the South and West lies a 329-mile
(529 km) border with Saudi Arabia. To the west
are the small Gulf states of Qatar and Bahrain,
while the UAE's adversary Iran lies just across
the water. A number of small islands stand
between them, and tensions sometimes flare
up over the ownership of two in particular:
Lesser and Greater Tunb.

There are no natural harbors along the UAE
coastline and fourteen manmade ones, the
biggest being Jebel Ali, which is the busiest port
in the Middle East. The UAE's waters are quite
rich in fish and marine life and it is possible
to see turtles, dolphins, and whale sharks,

in addition to edible local delicacies such as hammour and kingfish, although these species have been overfished in recent years. Historically fish represented the major form of protein for Emirati people, supplemented by the occasional mutton or goat.

There are some oases within the interior of the country, notably at Al Ain, which is known as "the garden city" for its greenery and natural hot springs. Here you can find an abundance of date palm trees, as well as mangoes and fig trees. Dates come into all Emirati meals in one form or another, and their stalks and leaves were once used in building local homes.

Much of the UAE's inland territory is still uninhabited. This doesn't mean that it is devoid of life, because the desert offers quite a variety of flora and fauna, but traveling in remote areas is not without risk. As well as the obvious dangers of desert scorpions, snakes, and spiders, sandstorms can make driving hazardous, and if it rains, flash floods can appear in mountain *wadis* (dry river beds). Do not attempt to travel alone into the desert or without informing people of where you are going.

Much of the UAE's biodiversity can also be found in its lush mangrove forests, which grow in abundance in Abu Dhabi, as well as dotted along the coastline between Dubai and the most-northern emirate Ras Al Khaimah.

Abu Dhabi is the largest Emirate geographically, and the majority of the oil and gas deposits that have so radically transformed Emirati society lie under its desert and coastal waters. While Dubai and Abu Dhabi have developed into sparkling metropolises, the oil wealth has trickled more slowly northwards through to the other Emirates. Umm al Quwain, Ras al Khaimah, and Ajman still had dirt roads and endured electricity outages until recently, and many people there still live in older style homes which seem a world away from the palatial Emirati villas of Abu Dhabi and Dubai.

CLIMATE

The climate of the UAE is principally hot and dry, reaching up to 109°F (43°C) on the coast and 115°F (46°C) in the interior. The hottest temperature ever recorded in the UAE is 125.7°F (52.1°C) in July 2002, but while most summer days are significantly cooler than that, it's the lethal combination of heat with high humidity that makes the UAE's summers feel so scorchingly sticky. When air conditioning first came to the UAE it must have seemed like a miraculous blessing to its people, who in the past would often venture inland in the summer, for example from Abu Dhabi to Al Ain, to escape the coastal humidity. Desert nights can be cool, but only in the deeper interior does this really have any noticeable impact.

The best time to visit the UAE is in the winter, between November and March, when temperatures range from 50°F (10°C) and 82.4°F (28°C). In the more mountainous Emirates of Fujairah and Ras al Khaimah, temperatures plunge much lower—it even snowed in Ras al Khaimah in February 2017, much to the delight of local children.

A blanket of thick fog descends on some winter mornings, which tends to cause plenty of chaos on the UAE's roads. The UAE also experiences the force of the "Shamal" winds in the spring and summer, blowing sand and dust particles up with it. The winds originate in Pakistan and blow through Iraq and Iran. It is advisable to stay indoors with all windows firmly closed during a sandstorm, particularly if you suffer from asthma.

RAIN

Average annual rainfall in the UAE is approximately 3.9 to 5.9 inches (99–150 mm), and it falls more frequently in the cooler mountainous regions of Fujairah and Ras Al Khaimah. Despite acute scarcity it has one of the highest per capita water usages globally. The UAE is keenly experimenting with cloud seeding technology, which appears to have significantly boosted its annual rainfall in recent years. This can be rather unsettling for the country's residents, who are never quite sure when it rains whether it is a natural occurrence, or a result of human intervention. Rain in the UAE tends to carry sand particles in it, which mean there are inevitably long queues at car washing stations when it stops.

The heavy rain that does fall naturally in the UAE, for about one week every year in December to February, is quite a cause for celebration, especially during years of widespread drought. However, most buildings appear to have been designed with the naïve presumption by the architect that it never rains heavily, which means that during storms, it rains inside, as well as outside. Schools and colleges will usually close, and because of an inadequate drainage on the roads, driving conditions can be hazardous.

Because the rainfall is subject to considerable variation, agricultural management can be difficult. Many traditional family farms are running out of groundwater, and are being abandoned. But some farmers are harnessing new technologies to solve the issue of water scarcity. At the Baniyas Center in Abu Dhabi, for example, traditional fish farming is undertaken through a system that uses the fish waste as a fertilizer for hydroponic vegetable tanks. There are even plans afoot to pull an iceberg all the way from Antarctica to Fujairah and convert it to fresh water, in order to ensure the UAE has enough water in the future.

THE ENVIRONMENT

The breakneck speed of the UAE's urban development would have been impossible without paying a hefty cost to the natural world. The last small stretch of sand dunes that still remains along the E11 road between Abu Dhabi and Dubai has already been earmarked for development, and desert campers have to travel ever further to get out of the UAE's sprawling megacities to find secluded spots. Oil slicks off the coast of

Fujairah are becoming a common occurrence, and although the UAE's hotel beaches are kept looking pristine by their staff, on undeveloped beaches, immense amounts of plastic are washed up, and volunteers are regularly roped in by local conservation groups to try to clean up the mess.

As well as its deserts and beaches, much of the UAE's biodiversity can be found in its mangroves forests. In recent years, the Abu Dhabi government has taken the initiative of planting thousands of mangrove saplings, to compensate for those uprooted to build waterside developments. Kayaking in the city's lush mangroves has become a popular pastime for tourists, but recent luxury developments on Abu Dhabi's Saadiyat and Yas Islands threaten the city's fragile mangrove eco-system with increased levels of pollution and noise.

The UAE's abundant supply of oil enables its bright city lights to keep burning, and its enormous malls to be luxuriously appointed and air-conditioned. Emirati citizens still have their energy costs heavily subsidized, although energy bills are now starting to creep up, especially for expatriates.

Bold steps are being taken to embrace alternative energy, and some of the world's largest solar farms have opened in the desert. Given the low price of gasoline in the UAE, visitors may be surprised at the number of charging points (around 200 in Dubai) for electric cars that are rapidly increasing in popularity. The country's first nuclear plant was expected to be operational in 2017 but has been rescheduled for 2018, with three more nuclear reactors scheduled to open by 2020.

All these environmentally friendly initiatives are not without good reason, for the UAE stands to face a catastrophic future if global warming continues at the rate some experts are predicting. In 2015, a study in the journal *Nature and Climate Change* cautioned that by the end of 2090,

temperatures in the UAE may become too hot
for human survival.

THE PEOPLE

The increase in population in the last forty years
has been so rapid that for those who have lived
through those years, the UAE is now virtually
unrecognizable. In 1975, the total population of the
Abu Dhabi Emirate was 211,812 people—merely
a fishing village—and in 2016, it was a global
metropolis with 2,908,173 residents, approximately
90 percent of whom were foreign workers and
their families.

Apart from the oasis city of Al Ain, the sleepy
desert towns of Madinat Zayed and Liwa, and
the accommodation settlements for oil industry
workers Al Ruwais and Delma Island, most people
live in the coastal cities, and those based in the
country's interior are mostly Pakistani and Indian
farm workers. While most Emirati families own
farms, they tend to only visit them at weekends or
in holidays, preferring to reside in their suburban
villas.

Because approximately 90 percent of the UAE's
population are non-Emirati citizens, visitors don't
always get the opportunity to interact with the
locals as almost all the country's hospitality staff
and shop assistants are foreign. The majority of the
UAE's residents are male who come from south

Asian countries (58 percent). Workers tend to be recruited on an ethnic basis according to the type of work required, with large cohorts of low-medium level office workers coming from Kerala in India, and manual laborers coming from Pakistan, Bangladesh, Sri Lanka, and Nepal. Filipinos do most of the retail and domestic jobs, and generally work at a lower level than their qualifications justify. Those in mid-managerial and technical occupations are usually recruited from Western countries, South Asia, and Arab countries, particularly Egypt and Jordan. The UAE is also increasingly recruiting from Africa, with teachers coming from South Africa, and security guards and taxi drivers from central African countries.

THE IMPORTANCE OF TRIBE

The Emirati people themselves are first and foremost tribespeople, and many of these tribes originated in Iran, Oman, Saudi Arabia, and Yemen. However, it is seen as a mark of status to be from a "pure" indigenous Emirati family, so if you ask an Emirati from where their descendants originated, you may encounter reluctance to broach the subject. Most Gulf Arabs residing within the borders of the country when independence was declared in 1971, or who had a suitably strong familial connection to a recognized citizen, were accorded citizenship and, in return, were expected to renounce previous political affiliations.

However, Emiratis are increasingly marrying outside of their own tribe and even nationality. In most cases, Emirati men are choosing to take a foreign wife as a second wife, or as an only wife if their first marriage ends in divorce. Some of the most successful Emirati business people are from marriages in which the father is Emirati and the mother is foreign, and some of them have felt that being half-caste has meant they have had to work harder in order to prove themselves worthy in their society. In 2012, Emirati filmmaker Amal Al-Agroobi shed light on the stigma attached to being "half-Emirati" in her controversial documentary of the same name.

A BRIEF HISTORY

Primitive hand axes discovered by archaeologists in Sharjah in 2011, thought to be 100,000 to 125,000 years old, are the earliest evidence of modern humans found anywhere outside Africa, and reveal that early man left Africa much early than previously thought.

In the remote past, Arabia as a whole had a climate with greater rainfall than it does today and agriculture was much more viable. The world's oldest *falaj* irrigation system (using underground water channels to water crops), thought to be 3,000 years old is located in Al Ain. The dry climate of Arabia seems to have stabilized in its current nature around five thousand years ago.

Trade flowed through Arabia from important centers such as Mecca from early times, and settlements from the Roman period show evidence of exchange of goods. Frankincense, an important trade good, was carried to Gaza and on to Europe. Eastward, trade routes had been established for thousands of years. Spices from the remote Indonesian islands have been found in the Syrian Desert and date to 2000 BCE, and at least one route passed through the desert, possibly utilizing territory now in the UAE. The most important state in Arabia between 1200 BCE and 275 CE was Saba, known in the west as Sheba (from the legend of the Queen of Sheba), with its capital at Ma'rib (in present day Yemen.) However, it is clear that a number of other smaller states existed and, from time to time, a king with pretensions to become known as a "unifier" emerged. It was more common, though, for tribes to live together in a state of autonomy. These tribes did not necessarily have a common ethnicity but instead represented a group of communities living in close proximity to each other, peaceably, and open to the outside world. Inscriptions and archaeological data reveal that the region was in contact with the Mediterranean states, Egypt, India, and cultures further afield.

In the centuries before the conquest of eastern Arabia by the Sassanian dynasty of southwestern Iran, from 223 CE to 651 CE, the area of the UAE witnessed the growth of local communities, crafts, coinage, and the development of language. The horse was first used at some period during the three centuries BCE, and the symbol of the Arabian horse has been held in great esteem in local culture ever since. During this time a variety of religious beliefs were held, including Christianity. Nestorian Christian monks built a monastery on Abu Dhabi's remote Sir Bani Yas Island in 600 CE. Thirty-two years later, envoys from the Prophet Mohammed brought Islam to the people of the Gulf Coast. The death of the Prophet led to a rebellion against his new religion, and one of the major battles was fought at Dibba in Fujairah. This was soon suppressed and Islam was exported overseas, using the base at Julfar (modern day Ras al Khaimah) to invade and convert Iran to the faith.

The export of Islam was extremely successful over the next centuries. Muslim courts of the period generally benefited from the wisdom of Islamic scholars and artists, and most rulers were patrons of art and culture. The standard of living in Islamic cities was among the highest in the world. However, different dynasties varied in their willingness to comply with this model and some rulers held more tyrannical ideas. The lives of the people of what is now the UAE continued to depend upon the commerce provided by the sea and its powerful neighboring rulers. The extent to which states could exert their influence over the nomadic Bedouin tribes of the interior was limited, because it was so difficult to travel there and to force people to abide by their laws.

In due course, European powers came to prominence in the Gulf as they sent out fleets to create colonies and improve trade with distant lands. The first to arrive in force were the Portuguese in the sixteenth century, driven by the desire to monopolize commerce in the Arabian Gulf. Dismayed by the stronghold on trade maintained by Muslims wherever they went, they blockaded the ports in the Arabian Gulf and elsewhere. This resulted in severe damage to many Muslim economies, including that of the UAE.

Piracy had been conspicuous in the Gulf for centuries, but the presence of enemies with a different religion multiplied the opportunities for attacks. The Emirati Al Qawasin pirate sheikhs created the Emirate of Ash-Shariqa, now known as Sharjah, as a base for pirate ships operating in the Gulf and beyond. Many modern Emiratis regard them as heroes who stood up to Western dominance.

In the sixteenth century, the Ottoman Turkish Empire succeeded the Egyptian Mamelukes as the preeminent Middle Eastern power, and Ottoman ships became active in the Gulf. The Ottomans did not govern Arabia directly, and a number of autonomous and semiautonomous sheikhs retained control of their local power bases.

Since much of Arabia is desert, in the empty space between coastal cities and oases, nomadic Bedouin tribes were able to move about more or less freely. They came into contact with settled people when it came to trade, when they were wanted as mercenaries, or when their paths crossed with those making the *Hajj p*ilgrimage to Mecca. A variety of religious schisms caused divisions through the centuries, the most important of which was the development of the Wahhabi tradition in central Arabia in the eighteenth century, which subsequently became extremely influential, particularly in Saudi Arabia. The majority of people on the Gulf Coast have continued to adhere to the "well-trodden path," and are described as Sunni Muslims. However, Wahhabi believers are more puritanical in their beliefs. By the beginning of the nineteenth century, Wahhabi power had become so great that the Ottoman leaders decided to take decisive military action against them. This resulted in the Ottoman occupation of western Arabia, but acceptance of Wahhabi dominance was recognized on the Gulf Coast. As Wahhabi rulers coalesced to create the Kingdom of Saudi Arabia, the Gulf Coast states retained political independence as Emirates to some extent because they were focused on the sea rather than the land.

The Al-Qawasin pirate sheikhs had skirmished with the British for some time as their control of India intensified. The British inflicted a naval defeat on the Qawasin fleet in 1819, which led to the dynasty's decline. The next powerbase was the Banu Yas tribal confederation, centered on the Abu Dhabi oases in Al Ain, which was land based rather than maritime in nature. The Al Nahyan faction, principally derived from the Al Bu Falah tribe, rose to become the dominant force in coastal politics, and it is the Al Nahyan clan in Abu Dhabi who rule the UAE today.

Three treaties helped establish the UAE as a discrete state: a 1820 peace treaty among the tribes; an 1853 treaty that established perpetual peace at sea; and a treaty signed in 1892 that restricted the Trucial States and their foreign relations entirely to the discretion of the British state, in return for protection against any attack. The Trucial Coast then became known as the Trucial States, continuing to include Bahrain and Qatar, until their independence from Britain was finally established in 1971.

In the nineteenth century, immigrants came mainly from India and Iran, to make the most of opportunities for international trading in the new port city of Dubai. While the British overlords largely ignored the States, providing such legal infrastructure as was necessary, migrants and indigenous people forged their own, individual culture based on trading and the desert.

The Japanese started producing cheaper, cultured pearls in 1921 and this, combined with the 1930s global depression, hit the UAE's pearl industry hard and resulted in a period of economic depression and famine. People were even paid in dates, as there was so little money to go around, and the average income in Dubai was just two rupees a day (a 8 ½ lb/3.9 kg) bag of sugar cost 30 rupees.) It was not until 1962 that oil from Abu Dhabi became the first to be exported from the county. From 1952, the Trucial States had established a semi-annual council, but relations with neighbors were not always peaceful. In 1952, the Saudis laid claim to the quiet oasis of Buraimi near the Omani border. When they were expelled three years later by British-led forces, Abu Dhabi retained six villages and Oman three, but tensions simmered between the Emiratis and the Saudis over the territory until 1974.

In 1968, the British announced the withdrawal of all their forces by the end of 1971, which stimulated negotiations among Trucial States leaders as to the formation of a unified state—the United Arab Emirates.

Negotiations were complex, and in 1971, when independence was achieved, both Bahrain and Qatar decided to establish independent states, while Abu Dhabi, Dubai, Sharjah, Fujairah, Ajman, and Umm al Quwain agreed to form the United Arab Emirates. The next year, Ras al Khaimah opted to join the UAE, having initially been reluctant to do so. The first president of the UAE was the widely respected leader of Abu Dhabi, Sheikh Zayed bin Sultan al Nahyan, who was subsequently re-elected to the post on five-year terms by the rulers of the individual Emirates, until his death in 2004.

SHEIKH ZAYED

Sheikh Zayed bin Sultan al Nahyan is still affectionately known by the people of the UAE as "the father of the nation," as he was the man who drew together the various tribes scattered across the seven Trucial States, unifying them to form one country in 1971.

That he achieved this feat peacefully is a tribute to his visionary leadership, and although he died in 2004, his legacy lives on in his people's lofty aspirations. It is his picture that is prominently displayed in the grounds of Emirates Palace along Abu Dhabi's main Cornice road for all those driving by to see. And whenever you enter a hotel in the

UAE, a picture of him can be seen hanging above the reception, usually accompanied by pictures of the current leader, Sheikh Khalifa, and also of the Sheikh of the particular Emirate in which the hotel is located.

Sheikh Zayed's understanding of the developmental needs of his people was astonishingly perceptive and revolutionized what was in living memory an undeveloped strip of barren land, with few apparent resources. Sheikh Zayed was born some time around 1918—birth dates were not then recorded—in Abu Dhabi. The youngest of four sons, he soon distinguished himself by his willingness to learn about the lives of his people, from the pearl fishers to the Bedouin tribes, from whom he developed a passion for falconry. He first took a leadership role in 1946, when he was appointed to govern the oasis villages of Al Ain and the adjoining desert region. From this post he developed his administrative skills and deepened his knowledge of the desert people.

Although oil had been discovered in Abu Dhabi in 1958, and exports began in 1962, under the reign of Sheikh Zayed's elder brother Sheikh Shakhbut bin Sultan al Nahyan before him, much of this new wealth was hidden away and Emiratis continued to live in poverty. Many still alive today recall having to drink dirty, brackish water dug out from the under the ground, and if a family member in Abu Dhabi become ill, a journey along dirt tracks to Dubai was necessary to reach the nearest hospital—assuming they were lucky enough to have access to a car.

This lack of progress led to frustration among members of the ruling family. Sheikh Zayed rose to power in a bloodless coup, allowing Sheikh Shakhbut to escape to Lebanon.

As a leader, Sheikh Zayed was characterized by his peaceful tolerance of other nationalities and his willing to learn from them, and also by his desire to bring the fruits of development to all the inhabitants of his country; including women. He is often quoted as saying: "The woman is half of society; any country which pursues development should not leave her in poverty or illiteracy." His point of view was ahead of his time in the Gulf region.

Sheikh Zayed increased contributions from Abu Dhabi to the Trucial States Development Fund as a means of enabling all Emiratis to profit from its oil wealth. At the same time, he was determined to preserve the culture of his people, and he introduced enduring initiatives aimed at educating young people into traditional ways of life. Looking both to the past and to the future, Sheikh Zayed achieved great things, as can be seen by comparing the progress of the UAE with that of some other oil-rich nations, which have instead gone down the routes of war and corruption.

SEVEN EMIRATES

Abu Dhabi

28,209 sq. miles (73,060 sq. km.) Pop. c. 2.784 million

The largest and richest Emirate. It is Abu Dhabi's oil wealth that has paid for most of the development of the entire country. Abu Dhabi is one of the most conservative socially of all the Emirates, particularly in the oasis town of Al Ain, which has preserved many of its traditional customs and includes an oasis which is a UNESCO world heritage site. In Abu Dhabi's remote desert towns of Madinat Zayed and Liwa, Emiratis still live relatively traditional Bedouin lifestyles and their grasp of English is not as strong as the city dwellers.

Ajman

100 sq. miles (260 sq. km.) Pop. c. 505,000

The smallest Emirate and now almost entirely urbanized, joining with neighbors Sharjah and Dubai as a potential megacity that is strongly reliant on tourism.

Dubai

1,583 sq. miles (4,100 sq. km.) Pop c. 2,885,000

Dubai city occupies a large part of this Emirate, and is the largest city of the federation, Dubai's strategic geographical location between the East and West has made it a popular stopover for tourists, and a bustling trading center.

Fujairah

444 sq. miles (1,150 sq. km.) Pop. c. 203,000

Fujairah is almost totally mountainous, and its limited economy is based on rock crushing, supplemented by state subsidies and tourism. With its coral reefs and turtles, Fujairah is the UAE's most popular destination for divers. The traditional culture and dialect of the people is distinct from that of much of the rest of the UAE, as it has been shaped by its reliance on the mountainous and valley farming as opposed to the nomadic rhythms of the desert. The Emirate is home to the UAE's oldest surviving mosque, Al Fadiyah, which is thought to date to the fifteenth century.

Sharjah

1,004 sq. miles (2,600 sq. km.) Pop. c. 1,400,000

Sharjah has a 5,000-year history of early settlements and its scholarly leader, Sheikh Sultan bin Muhammad Al Qasimi (who has a PhD in history from Exeter University), has been keen to promote its architecture and traditional conservative culture. It is the only Emirate where alcohol is banned.

Ras al Khaimah

656 sq. miles (1,700 sq. km.) Pop.c. 300,000

For most of its history, Ras al Khaimah was part of the Ash-Shariqah Emirate (Sharjah) and was ruled by the Qawasin pirate sheikhs. This Emirate is now making the most of its rugged mountains, hot springs, and copper-tinted sand dunes by investing heavily in tourism.

Umm al Quwain

301 sq. miles (780 sq. km.) Pop. c. 72,000

Umm al Quwain is the least populated Emirate, It was also part of Ash-Shariqah and its economy was based on both piracy and pearl diving. Visitors can enjoy its sprawling mangrove forests and water park, "Dreamland Aquapark."

MODERN TIMES

Income from oil exports continued to grow, especially after the increases in oil prices in the 1970s. In the early part of the decade, the price of oil quadrupled as the Organization of Petroleum Exporting Countries (OPEC), of which the UAE was a member, took advantage of the rapid expansion of economic development around the world and the accompanying increase in demand for oil. This increase, which caused a dramatic realignment of global political power and influence, was also closely related to the issue of Arab–Israel relations, since the majority of OPEC members were Islamic countries from the Middle East. The ability of the UAE government to bring about the economic and social development of the country was thereby greatly enhanced.

The long building boom that was sparked has continued until this day and, as the economy becomes more diversified, seems set to continue. However, this was possible only because of national unity, which was far from assured in the 1970s. Dubai and Ras al Khaimah, in particular, were resistant to federal control of their individual affairs, and a dispute between the ruling families of Dubai and Sharjah in the late 1970s led to each side's armored personnel carriers facing off against each other. The crucial breakthrough occurred when Sheikh Rashed of Dubai agreed to become prime minister and vice president of the UAE in 1979, signaling the end of Dubai's resistance to the process of federalization. Many of the people from the other Emirates meanwhile, have become marginalized in political terms as Abu Dhabi's oil wealth subsidizes their own more meagre economies.

Whereas the UAE's relationship with Iran can best be described as one of "mutual distrust," the UAE has long held a close bond with their "brothers" in Saudi Arabia, with whom they share religious ties and face the same long-term issues of how to wean their economies off reliance on oil money and manage large foreign populations. Political changes in the region triggered by the Arab Spring and the rise of ISIS have prompted the UAE and Saudi Arabia to forge a stronger partnership, and to take a more emboldened role in regional politics. National service was introduced for young Emirati males in 2014. Since 2015, Saudi Arabia and the UAE have been fighting a proxy war against Iran by deploying troops to fight in Yemen against the Houthis, and since June 2017, the UAE and Saudi Arabia have broken off diplomatic ties with their neighbors Qatar, who they accuse of harboring extremists. But the UAE's increasing influence on the world stage is not just down to its military maneuverings and political posturing against Qatar and Iran, but also the benevolent way it spends its wealth to help those in crisis overseas. According to a 2017 report by the Organization for Economic Co-operation and Development (OECD), the UAE spends more on foreign aid—most notably to Africa and Yemen—than any other nation on earth compared to its wealth. However, because of its strict visa system, the UAE does not accept refugees.

GOVERNMENT AND POLITICS

The UAE is a federation in which the seven

individual Emirates retain certain powers for themselves, while a federal government oversees state-level policy, such as foreign affairs and defense. On the death of the founding father and president Zayed bin Sultan al Nahyan in 2013, the presidency passed to the next ruler of Abu Dhabi, President Khalifa bin Zayed al Nahyan.

THE SHEIKHS

The ruling style of the conservative Al Nahyan family in Abu Dhabi differs considerably to the more liberal-minded Al Maktoums in Dubai.

While several of the Al Maktoum women are under the media spotlight playing sports at international level, including show jumping, polo, skydiving, karate, and taekwondo, the more conservative al Nahyan wives and daughters shun the public eye. President Sheikh Khalifa is rumored to be ill and rarely makes public appearances anymore, and it is his younger brother, Sheikh Mohammed bin Zayed al Nahyan, who is Abu Dhabi's Sandhurst-educated crown prince and the revered public face of Abu Dhabi. Dubai's charismatic leader and the UAE's prime minister, Sheikh Mohammed bin Rashid al Maktoum, is held in high esteem, not just by Dubai's Emiratis, but by it's expatriate population too. While he is known for his love of horse racing and his close relationship with the British royal family, in Dubai, he is a man of the people, who has been known to ride the metro and give blood to set an example to others.

THE FEDERAL SUPREME COUNCIL

The highest authority in the land is the Federal
Supreme Council (FSC), which is composed of the
seven rulers of the individual Emirates and which
meets on a quarterly basis to decide high-level
issues. The FSC votes for the posts of president
and vice president. The rulers of Abu Dhabi and
of Dubai are recognized as the most important
members of the FSC, and they can veto decisions if
necessary; however, the leaders prefer there to be a
show of unity, and any controversial decisions are
customarily settled in private.

Historically, Arab rulers have appointed advisors
to serve as part of their council in a *majlis*, and
the Federal National Council (FNC) in Abu
Dhabi continues this tradition. The FNC has forty
members, half appointed by the individual rulers of
each Emirate and half voted
by members of an electoral
college. But this democracy
is limited, as electoral
college members must be
appointed by the ruler.
The electoral college has
6,689 members, 14 percent
of whom are women. A
female candidate from
Abu Dhabi, Dr Amal Al
Qubaisi, became the first to
claim a seat in the FNC and

is the region's first female leader of a national assembly, representing a historic moment for Arab women's political empowerment.

Voting intentions are influenced by tribal and familial links as well as policy stances. The FNC is permitted to review policy and comment upon it, but has no power to amend it or to introduce legislation independently.

According to the government, there is no need for political parties or leaders, since all necessary debate takes place through the FSC, the rulers' palace *majlis* or FNC. If political parties were to arise, it is likely that there would be some pressure to create parties based on tribal allegiances and religion, and this could prove divisive. Religious extremism has a logic that appeals to some people, and the state is anxious about its potential influence. The Muslim Brotherhood, the Islamic political party that has gained popularity across the region in recent years, was branded a terrorist group in the UAE in 2014 and many of its supporters have been jailed.

THE COURTS

Laws in the UAE are upheld by judges appointed by the president. Individual Emirates have their own courts to deal with civil, criminal, and commercial cases, as well as Islamic courts to administer cases involving family or moral issues, according to Sharia law.

Some judicial decisions have aroused controversy in cases where the subjects are non-Muslim, particularly in child custody cases in which, according to Sharia law, the husband or nearest living male relative is bestowed custody. However, in 2017, judges in Abu Dhabi signed an agreement with Christian clergy giving churches jurisdiction to approve marriages, mediate divorces, and handle child custody, thereby enabling the UAE's non-Muslim population to skip Sharia law judgement.

INTERNATIONAL AFFILIATIONS

The UAE is a full member of the International Monetary Fund (IMF), the International Labor Organization (ILO), the Group of 77 (G-77), the United Nations (UN), and the Organization of Petroleum Exporting Countries (OPEC). The UAE is also a member of the Gulf Cooperation Council (GCC), a political and economic alliance that it formed in 1981 alongside Qatar, Kuwait, Bahrain, Oman, and Saudi Arabia. Until political tensions began bubbling up against Qatar in 2017 over accusations that Qatar had been sponsoring terrorist groups, the GCC had proven itself to be a fairly effective forum for diplomacy, agreeing for example on a framework for imposing a goods and service tax (VAT) on its citizens in 2018. But not all GCC agreements have been adhered to. Plans put in place in 2011 for a rail network linking member states appear to have stalled, due to the slump in oil prices.

In December 2017, the UAE announced a new economic and military alliance with Saudi Arabia, forging a "joint co-operation committee" between the two powers, and thereby further weakening the political influence of the GCC.

THE ECONOMY

The impact of oil money is present in every aspect of UAE society. It is estimated that Abu Dhabi, which holds the bulk of the UAE's oil reserves, is the world's third largest exporter of crude oil and has the fifth largest natural gas reserve. Oil and gas are extracted by a variety of joint ventures between UAE government oil companies, together with large foreign oil companies. The foreign companies provide technical and technological competence, while the local partners offer access to the oil fields.

The economy of Abu Dhabi has until recently been almost entirely dependent upon the presence of offshore oil and gas. But things are changing. 2016 was the year when the impact of sustained low oil prices hit the Abu Dhabi economy hard, and tens of thousands of oil and gas jobs were lost. The government has been trying to speed up the diversification of the economy, with aspiring entrepreneurs being helped to set up companies, for example through free start-up incubator programs held at New York University's Abu Dhabi campus. As a result of government efforts to diversify the economy, non-oil sectors now account for 70 percent of the UAE's GDP. It is not known exactly how many years worth of oil the UAE has left: accounts vary from between 40 and 140 years.

At present, the UAE's economic outlook remains uncertain. Dubai's economy is somewhat buffered by increased government spending on infrastructure projects designed to prepare the Emirate for the 2020 World Expo that it is organizing, but other Emirates are starting to see cracks in their economic plans. In 2015, Abu Dhabi had the second highest residential rent in the world, but rental prices have been dropping as the market stagnates, and job losses and lower wages prompt more foreign workers to leave.

The government's plan is to achieve sustainable economic diversity for Abu Dhabi by 2030. To help achieve this, a "sin" tax on soda, tobacco, and energy drinks was introduced in October 2017, and three months later, VAT was introduced at a rate of 5 percent. Other taxes are also now under consideration.

Abu Dhabi is also investing in infrastructure projects spanning the globe, through its sovereign wealth fund (the world's second largest), the Abu Dhabi Investment Authority (ADIA), which is estimated to have assets of more than USA $800 billion. Approximately 40 percent of all oil revenues are reinvested through ADIA into strategic industries such as hotels, airports, and high-value real estate. At home, in order to lure in more tourists, Abu Dhabi has been heavily investing in futuristic theme parks, museums, and art galleries, such as Louvre Abu Dhabi, which opened in 2017 to much fanfare.

It is rumored that even if the oil revenues were to stop immediately, the profits flowing from investments that have already been made are sufficient to ensure that no Emirati citizen alive today need ever work again.

GOVERNMENT GENEROSITY

Emirati citizens are looked after by a generous welfare system, which was built up by Sheikh Zayed in the 1970s to ensure that the new-found oil wealth was distributed fairly among his people. This means Emiratis have access to free healthcare (and despite the high standard of healthcare in the UAE, this even covers most operations abroad), subsidized fuel, electricity, and water, generous government-funded retirement plans, plots of land, free higher education, and a Dh 70,000 grant given to Emirati men when they marry an Emirati woman. The UAE's generous leaders also pay the debts of Emirati nationals to mark public holidays.

But generosity has its limits. In 2016, Sheikh Mohammed bin Rashid al Maktoum carried out a surprise spot check of civil service departments and when he found empty desks, nine senior Emirati officials lost their jobs. In a country that attributes a high value on honor, this highly publicized move sent a powerful message to Emiratis that idleness would not be tolerated.

Compulsory military service, which was introduced in 2014, has also been sharpening the work ethic of young Emirati males. Having seen the after-effects of the Arab Spring in other Middle Eastern countries, the UAE's leaders are acutely aware of the dangers of a restless unemployed youth.

TREATMENT OF FOREIGN WORKERS

There are three main cohorts of the expatriate society: those (usually Westerners) who come for the adventure of exploring a new country and for possible short-term financial gain. There

are the families from war-torn and politically
compromised countries such as Libya, Yemen,
and Syria, who hang onto their time in the UAE
for as long as they can because they are scared
for the future of their own country. Finally, there
are the workers who have left their families in
India, Pakistan, the Philippines, Bangladesh, and
other developing countries to build and service
the city. This third group usually live in so-called
labor camps out in the desert. Their motivations
for coming to the UAE are purely financial, and
they speak with pride about how they are paying
to educate their children back home. After
spending their days building and maintaining
the UAE's shiny new towers, malls, and luxury
hotels, these workers are transported back to
their crude accommodation in buses that often
lack air conditioning.

Emiratis are very sensitive to criticism about
their treatment of foreign workers, and the
UAE government has done a lot to combat the
negative image in the international press of men
being herded into inhumane living conditions.
While working outdoors during the blistering
summer heat must be unimaginably tough for
construction workers, the law nowadays prohibits
them from having to work in the hottest hours
of the day between 12.30 p.m. and 3.00 p.m.
from May to September. Conditions in the newer
camps have improved in recent years, with sites

such as Saadiyat Construction Village and Industrial City Abu Dhabi (ICAD) boasting facilities such as a cricket ground, library, a movie theater, markets, and parks. But the older camps still remain. At Sonapur, a mega-camp housing some 200,000 men on the outskirts of Dubai, men sleep ten to twelve in each room in prison-like concrete buildings. A drive into the UAE's industrial areas, such as Mussafah in Abu Dhabi and in Jebel Ali in Dubai, often feels like entering a bleak post-apocalypse world, devoid of green landscaping, and with rubbish strewn by the sides of the roads. Fights occasionally break out at the camps between different nationalities, as living in such close proximity is a cause of considerable stress.

Investors mostly appreciate the UAE government's *laissez-faire* attitude toward the welfare of its workers, who have little hope of appeal against unfair employers. But recent laws have sought to stamp out unreasonable treatment. It used to be the case that workers without a job had just 48 hours to find employment before they had to leave the UAE, but now they have thirty days. In addition, new rules governing how the visa-sponsorship operates introduced in 2016 should theoretically make it easier for workers to change employers before their contract ends if their rights are violated. However, some unscrupulous employers still hold the passports of their employees who are too afraid of repercussions to fight back.

THE QUANDARY OF LONG-TERM EXPATRIATES

Of all the Emirates, Dubai in particular has been successful in forging a community of long-term (mostly Indian) expatriate families, who feel a sense of belonging to Dubai, and a genuine affection for the city they call home. But Emirati citizenship is closely guarded, and the visa system ensures that foreigners are only welcome in their "home" as long as they are working. The visa system works well for short-term visitors, who come to the UAE for the climate, the outdoors lifestyle, and the chance to save more money than they would do at home. But second generation expatriates whose parents brought them up in the UAE live under the shadow of knowing that if they lose their jobs and cannot find new ones within thirty days, they will be cast out back to a "home" country in which they have never lived, and may not have any close family or friends there to welcome them. This can be a difficult issue to address, as freedom of expression is limited. Those with substantial assets in the UAE can apply for residency, but for those less well placed financially and whose home country is Syria, Yemen, or Somalia, the future can look bleak. They may then be willing to accept poor working conditions for little pay, in order to stay with their families in the only country they know as home.

Since the UAE is only forty-six years old, these expatriates are the first generation to face this problem. As Abu Dhabi and Dubai become major draws for culture in the region, these citizenship issues may need to be re-examined.

BIDOUNS

The bidouns are "stateless" people who were born in the UAE, but have not officially been granted Emirati nationality and therefore cannot appreciate its perks, such as medical insurance and free college education. Bidouns, whose parents often came from Iran or other GCC countries, number between 10,000 and 100,000 in the UAE. Most hold passports from the Comoros Islands, although they have never lived there, because it enables them to hold some form of official identity. The Bidoun tend to be relatively poor because they cannot claim an Emirati-level salary, and as a result can lead them to become involved in criminal activity. In some cases, their resentment leads them to political crimes against the state.

THE CONTRAST BETWEEN OLD AND NEW IN DUBAI

Dubai Creek runs through what, until recently, used to be the heart of Dubai, but massive developments along the coast have meant that this area is today often overlooked. Instead tourists are lured to New Dubai's latest manmade architectural triumph: the Dubai Water Canal, a 2-mile (3.2 km) long canal that starts at Business Bay and is designed to give waterfront views and pedestrian walkways to shiny new hotels and restaurants.

Today the old creek is almost all that remains of old Dubai, and a bid is underway to give this

8 ½-mile (13 km) strip between Bur Dubai and
Deira UNESCO world heritage status. The pace
of life is slower here. It is a place where people like
to gather to stroll or drink coffee while watching
the quaint wooden *abra* boats, chugging their
way back and forth across the water. The cargo
boats are *dhows,* a form of the one-masted trading

MUHAMMED ALI'S VISIT TO ABU DHABI

It's a little known fact that back in 1969,
when Abu Dhabi was a backwater fishing
village, and before the Emirates had unified
to form a country, the great American boxer
Muhammad Ali chose to visit. At that time in
his life, the three-time world boxing champion
had been stripped of his boxing title and
barred from the ring, after refusing to fight in
the Vietnam war, saying he had "no quarrel"
with the Vietcong. He was said to have been
on the way back from Mecca after performing
his first *Hajj*, when he stopped off in Abu
Dhabi. Ali wanted to visit a desert greenhouse
planting project being run at the time by the
University of Phoenix, perhaps inspired by
the notion of mankind being able to green the

vessels used by Arabs for centuries to carry goods up and down the coast. Most commercial vessels have shifted their base up the creek to Deira, where thousands of *dhows* offload cargo from Iran, Somalia, Yemen, India, and other countries in the region.

desert. Photographs from the time testify that Ali met with Sheikh Zayed and his sons, and came back to Abu Dhabi in 1974 as a guest of Sheikh Zayed.

Ali also fought several boxing matches in Dubai, reportedly in order to raise money to pay for mosques to be built back in the USA. But it is his trips to Abu Dhabi that are more extraordinary simply because this was a period before other international celebrities had even heard of Abu Dhabi, never mind visited. Unfortunately, Ali's impressions about what he thought of Abu Dhabi and its people have been lost in time. But Ali's tolerant, peaceful brand of Islam certainly would have chimed with the world Sheikh Zayed was trying to build in Abu Dhabi at the time.

VALUES &
ATTITUDES

The values and attitudes of Emirati people are shaped
by three factors: Islam, Arab, and Bedouin traditions;
the desert environment; and the impact of having
money and power in a country where roughly
90 percent of the populace are foreign.

Owing in part to its proximity to the sacred
cities of Mecca and Medina, the UAE has been
suffused with Islamic influence for much more
than a thousand years. Life in the desert often meant
intense competition for the scarce resources. It
shaped characters that were strong-willed and
fearlessly resilient. The separation of family units and
tribal groupings from other communities by difficult
terrain has inspired the creation of elaborate and vital
rules for hospitality, and a protocol for negotiation.

Emiratis generally define themselves in terms
of their family or tribe first, their Emirate second,
country third, and Arab world fourth. After all, only
half a century ago, the Bedouin moved their flocks
from one grazing area to another as they followed
the rain, owing allegiance to the strongest leader,
and territory on a map had little meaning to them.
The government is making considerable efforts to

promote the nation as the basis of personal identity, but old loyalties are slow to disappear.

When wealth is more or less equally distributed, social relations are conducted on an equitable basis. However, now that Emirati people are much wealthier than the more numerous migrant workers in their country, they have become accustomed to consider foreigners to be employees who might represent some sort of threat to their sense of national identity, and more social occasions have become off-limits to expatriates. Long-term expatriates recall that when Dubai and Abu Dhabi were more like villages than global cities, more mingling between the Emiratis and Western population took place. During Eid for example, it was normal for British wives to visit local households and pay their respects. As the number of foreigners has increased, Emirati society has closed ranks and it has become more difficult for outsiders to integrate. In fact, it is quite possible for a visiting worker to live in the UAE for a year and never have occasion to speak to an Emirati.

There are several factors that prohibit socialization: Because Emirati males and females have separate *majlis* living areas, couples tend to socialize separately with their respective friends. Equally, some Emiratis would feel uncomfortable attending a social occasion with where alcohol is being served. But expatriates, who do respectfully make the effort to engage with locals on occasions when it is possible to do so, find them to be most obliging, and cultural similarities are often greater than any differences.

THE BUBBLE MENTALITY

While the UAE is multicultural, it achieves this through more of a "salad bowl" than "melting pot" mentality. Expatriates sometimes feel as though they are living in a cultural bubble, which only ever merges with people who share the same life perspectives and cultural backgrounds as they do.

If you are a parent, the bubble mentality can be broken through your children. Emirati women love to make a big fuss over young children of every nationality, and in public settings, Emirati and expatriate families can often share a joke about a particular child's amusing antics. For women, beauty salons offer opportunities to strike up conversation with Emirati customers in for a manicure. For men, the best cultural icebreaker is football, which Emirati men are usually passionate about.

STATUS AND SOCIAL STRUCTURE

The social system is hierarchically inflexible so due to their nationality, the lowest paid expatriates find it difficult to work their way up the career ladder. One adage that Emiratis occasionally use is "to be as clever as an Egyptian," which illustrates how foreigners are often met with preconceptions about their role and status in society based on broad ethnic generalization. Visitors should be aware that, based on their ethnicity, there will be some expectations of what kind of person they are, the type of work they do, and, consequently, their social status.

Moving from being an outsider to an insider is likely to be a lengthy process without personal connections. Those who achieve this will find there are subtle, unstated, and longstanding distinctions in status within Emirati society. On the surface, the class structure that permeates other countries might not seem to exist as almost all Emiratis are required to attend university, no matter how unacademically inclined they might be, and very few could be said to live in poverty. The fact that almost all Emiratis wear their national dress in public also makes it difficult to differentiate them apart to foreigners based on class.

But there are marked differences between those who obtained their degrees overseas (the USA is the most popular destination), who tend to be fluent English speakers with more of an international mindset, and those who were wholly educated in the UAE. There are also distinctions between those whose family were desert nomads before the advent of modern development, and those who were farmers, fishermen, and tradespeople. In Dubai, which was a bustling trade port, the women often worked on market stalls while the men fished, which might explain why women from Dubai appear more liberal than those from other Emirates.

There are also distinctions between rural and urban Emiratis, between "pure" Emiratis and those with some foreign heritage, and between those from different Emirates, based on their different dialects, cuisines, and customs. The Emirati stereotype in the British tabloid newspapers is of people who own flats in London's exclusive boroughs, and park their Lamborghinis outside Harrods department store. But although it's common for Emiratis to spend their long hot summer abroad, only a small, super-wealthy elite has the money for a luxurious second home in central London.

FAMILY

The family, which is related to tribe, remains the basic social structure and, no matter how far members may roam, they will always be aware of their roots in the familial home. Although public schools are free for Emiratis, some local children attend private international schools in order to sharpen their English. But while children of other nationalities regularly interact outside of school on play dates, it is more common for Emirati children, outside of school, to socialize with their cousins and siblings.

As they grow up, Emiratis are also made painfully aware that any fond friendships they do nurture with expatriates are bound to be short-lived, because one day they inevitably return home. This inherent transiency makes Emiratis naturally more inclined to seek out deeper and more long-lasting relationships with their own kind.

ARAB PRIDE

Emiratis are proud of their Arab heritage. It was the Arabs who were blessed to receive the Prophet

Mohammed and, hence, the message known as the Islamic religion. This was delivered to Mohammed by the Angel Gabriel in the Arabic language, which is believed to be the language of heaven. Spurred by this message, Arab armies conquered and inspired the conversion to Islam of people from Spain in the west to Indonesia in the east, via all the many countries in between, which is a proud, distinguished heritage. Arabs and other Muslims may be different ethnically, but the shared memory of their Islamic past is a badge of pride that unites them.

The tide of history had changed by the twentieth century, however, and Arabs and Muslims generally were subjected to the depredations of Western colonialism. The humiliation that people felt as a result of being colonized was intensified when it became clear just what reserves of oil were available to those who controlled their territories. Arabs often draw a parallel between British control of the oil fields prior to the Second World War and the American-led invasion of Iraq, which appeared to be for the same motivation.

Clearly, there is scope for enormous levels of very heated debate about these issues, in which the role of Israel is customarily involved. Visitors would do well to bear in mind the history of exploitation, on top of ancient glory, that their Arab friends will bring to their side of any debate. Emiratis control the power within most social forms of interaction, so it is polite to listen to what one's hosts have to say.

CHARITY

Generosity is deeply engrained into Emirati culture.
Many a foreign resident has a tale to tell of a time
when their car got stuck in the sand, and was towed
to safety by Emirati strangers, who refused to accept
money as a gesture of thanks.

Islam places a great deal of stress on charity, and
many charitable foundations exist to collect donations
and redistribute them to the needy. Muslims are
expected to give 2.5 percent of their income away to
charity every year, after paying for basic needs such
as food, clothing, and housing, in private donations
known as *zakat*. The elaborately decorated new
mosques that have been built on almost every street
of the Emirates have usually been paid for in *zakat*.

Due to a fear that charity funds might find their
ways into the wrong hands, the UAE has implemented
stringent laws that only permit residents to donate to
charities with a license to do so, such as the Emirates
Red Crescent. This has caused some expatriate-
organized charity events, such as school jumble sales
and sponsored marathons, to be canceled for fear of
breaking the law.

RELIGION

The sound of the muezzin calling Muslims to pray
can be heard blasting out from mosque loudspeakers
almost everywhere in the UAE, and it is a constant
reminder to foreign visitors that Islam is the religion
of the UAE. Islam came into being through Prophet

Mohammed in the seventh century CE. According to Islamic belief, Mohammed was visited by the Angel Gabriel, who recited to him the holy word of God, which was subsequently written down and became known as the Koran. God's intention was for Mohammed to be the final in the succession of prophets who had been sent to Earth, including Adam, Noah, Abraham, Moses, and Jesus, all of whom are revered as holy prophets in their own right. However, as the final prophet, the message of Mohammed superseded that of all the others and, consequently, the Koran explains exactly how humans should live. The term "Islam" itself literally means "submission," and Muslims believe that they are submitting themselves continually to the will of God.

Islam combines within itself both the spiritual realm and the temporal realm, and consequently

THE FIVE PILLARS OF ISLAM

The Five Pillars of Islam represent the very foundations of the religion and provide structure to the daily life of Muslims.

- The first is the Shahadah, or profession of faith. This is the belief that there is no God but Allah and Mohammed is His Prophet. Making this profession categorizes a person as a member of the Muslim community.

- The second pillar is the five-times-daily prayers. All Muslims must listen out for the muezzin who will issue the call to prayer five times each day. This is the signal for the faithful to wash themselves and pray in the prescribed way. In mosques, women and men have separate sections. If it is not convenient for a man to visit a mosque for prayers, he may line up his prayer mat so it is facing Mecca to make his prayers, and visitors to the UAE may notice groups of Pakistani and

many Muslims believe that the rulers of countries should be religious leaders, not politicians or nonreligious leaders. The leadership of the UAE has to date managed to keep separate the two realms and,

Arab men on scraps of grass by busy streets, kneeling on their prayer mats. Take note that prayers cannot be completed if a woman is in view or walks in front of the praying men.

- The third pillar of Islam is the tax of *zakat*, or purification. Islamic thought considers the paying of interest on money lent to be a sin, which has given rise to Islamic banks offering a variety of schemes to avoid paying interest.

- The fourth pillar is fasting during the month-long period of Ramadan, when Muslims should refrain from refreshments during daylight hours.

- The final pillar is the requirement to go on the *Hajj*, which is the pilgrimage to Mecca. These days, the proximity of the UAE to Mecca and the transportation links make this a much less onerous trip than it once was, and so nearly everyone is able to fulfill this tenet at least once.

as a result, has governed the state through political perspectives.

Muslims always accompany the mention of the name of the Prophet Mohammed with the words

"Peace Be Upon Him." Generally, Islamic thought precludes the representation of human beings in any form of art, as this would be disrespectful to God's work in creating the original people. In particular, there is a very strong taboo accompanying the portrayal of Mohammed. In 2015, cartoons representing the Prophet led to angry demonstrations around the world. As a visitor, it's best not to use humor when discussing religion, so as not to be misunderstood.

The UAE'S Churches

As well as its five thousand mosques, the UAE has more than forty churches, and the number keeps growing. In the area of Al Mushrif in Abu Dhabi, colloquially known as "church area," on a Friday, you can enjoy the gospel singing of Ethiopian women outside St Andrews Anglican Church, the imam at the mosque next door delivering his sermon, and the priest saying mass in the next-door Catholic St Josephs Church. What is remarkable is that this mosque was deliberately built to stand between these churches, to safeguard them against a terrorist bombing. The mosque's grand white domed structure is the biggest mosque on Abu Dhabi Island. In 2017, it was renamed the "Mary, Mother of Jesus" mosque to stand as a poignant symbol to the world of the UAE's religious tolerance.

ATTITUDES TOWARD WOMEN

According to a combination of Koranic and traditional beliefs, Emiratis believe that men and women should be kept separate from each other most of the time. This is because they will be tempted into sins of improper intimacy if they are allowed to be together. To prevent this from happening, the best solution is to keep women covered up.

Before the advent of oil wealth, women more commonly worked outside the house and were not required to cover their bodies to the extent that they are now. According to some, it was the presence of so many male migrant workers that persuaded Emirati men to insist that the women protect themselves by wearing the *abaya* (full-length outer garment) and *shayla* (head covering).

Sheikh Zayed understood the need to protect Emirati women, but also thought it would be necessary to provide opportunities for those who wished to work outside the household. Achieving this necessitated the creation of workplaces in which women could perform without exposing themselves to possible criticism.

In the more conservative area of Al Ain, all-female call centers were opened by Abu Dhabi Commercial Bank and Etihad Airways so women could be given the chance to work without having to interact with men.

It is now considered the norm for Emirati females to go to university (although only a small number are permitted to study abroad), and then to work in a chosen career upon their graduation. Despite cuts in federal public spending of 27 percent in 2015, as a result of the fall in oil prices, Emirati rulers are still investing in education, encouraging women, in particular, to study. In 1975, shortly after oil was discovered, only 38 percent of Emirati women over the age of fifteen could read or write. Today, that figure is 92 percent, compared with 90 percent for men.

The glass ceiling has been shattered in the last decade in many jobs that were thought of as being for men only, and now the country takes pride in its Emirati female aircraft pilots, opera singers, ice skaters, and martial artists. While in the past, women might have been expected to give up work upon having children, nowadays most Emirati career women leave young children at workplace nurseries, or at home with their maids. But not every family agrees with allowing females to perform in traditionally male jobs, and the progress is by no means irreversible.

The leader of Dubai, Sheikh Mohammed bin Rashid al Maktoum is particularly passionate about women's advancement. In 2012, he made it compulsory for companies and government agencies to appoint women to their boards of directors, saying that women had "proved themselves" and needed to take part in decision-making. Since then, women have also taken up front role positions in government, including their Minister of State for Happiness, Ohood al Roumi. In 2015, the government established a gender-balanced council to ensure that Emirati women continued to play a leading

role in the development of the country.

Segregation of the sexes still occurs in the Emirati public primary and secondary school system, and at university level, however steps are now being taken to allow females onto what were previously all-male campuses, for example at Abu Dhabi Men's College. This interaction means that when males and females need to collaborate in the workplace, they are more comfortable in doing so.

Though it is still taboo for the males and females to have a romantic relationship before marriage, young male and female Emiratis can be seen holding hands in shopping malls, particularly in more liberal Dubai, where this would have been frowned upon a decade ago. Another sign of how gender roles are changing is the sight of fathers pushing their children's strollers in the park.

It is worth noting that while Emirati women love to take photographs of themselves and each other on their cell phones, it is polite to check first before photographing them yourself. There will probably be an understanding between the women that their photographs are only shared on private, female-only social media accounts.

Having sex with somebody with whom you are not married is also a crime, and in some cases, women who have reported a rape to police have found themselves being charged for this offense.

ALCOHOL

There exists a dangerous paradox between the glitz and glamor of the UAE's nightlife scene, and the realities of the conservative Sharia legal system. Buying alcohol is technically illegal in the UAE unless you first obtain an alcohol license, and this is only available to non-Muslim residents. Behaving in a drunken manner in public is a crime, and although police tend to turn a blind eye to tourists drinking in clubs and bars, the moment they come out onto the streets and into taxis, they could be arrested for inappropriate behavior. Realistically, such arrests are rare, and the police don't seem to go out on patrol actively seeking to arrest people for being drunk. However, if a person should require police assistance, and they happen to have been drinking alcohol, they could then be charged for that.

COVERING UP

As the UAE has welcomed increasing numbers of foreign tourists into their country, Emiratis have had to accept that some of those tourists choose to wear clothes that they deem to be inappropriate. Signs have been put up in shopping malls advising on appropriate clothing, which for men usually means no shorts, and women are expected to cover up their cleavage, shoulders and only wearing skirts that come below the knees. But the message doesn't appear to be getting through. If you walk through almost any mall in Dubai, and many in Abu Dhabi, you are bound to see foreign women dressed in tight vest tops, short skirts or dresses which local women would disapprove of. The sight of these scantily-clad women creates some tension and misunderstandings between the Emiratis and the expatriate community, and I recommend any visitor to the UAE to be sensitive to the local culture when choosing their wardrobe. Kissing in public is also taboo.

MARRIAGE

Marriages between suitable members of different families are one of the most common means of extending social networks. Traditionally, the prospective groom's mother is tasked with finding her son a suitable bride. Although today couples can connect on social media before they meet face to face, courtship does not usually begin until after the marriage contract, or *milcha* is signed. Then a couple can get to know each other, chaperoned by relatives. A wedding party takes place some weeks or months later, after which the marriage is consummated.

Islamic law in the UAE allows polygamy, with men permitted to marry up to four wives, as long as each is treated equally. However, in reality, a man must be quite wealthy to be able to afford to maintain more than one wife, and the norm is to have one wife at a time. Divorce in the UAE has been on the rise, as it has worldwide. Figures from the UAE's National Bureau of Statistics show that since 2008, about 40 percent of Emirati marriages end in divorce. A UAE-wide 2016 study by Zayed University, UAE University, and Al Khwarizmi International College found that interference of family members, social media usage, financial issues, and lack of communication were some of the biggest factors to marital breakdowns.

It is a sensitive subject, but increasing numbers of Emirati men are choosing to take foreign wives; perhaps because the dowry and wedding expenses the families have to pay when marrying an Emirati woman are in some cases prohibitive. According to Judicial Department statistics of the Emirate of Abu Dhabi there were 5,892 new marriage contracts registered in 2016 and in only 3,327 of these, the wife was an Emirati citizen. Muslim Emirati men are free to marry non-Muslim women, if they are "people of the book"—Christians or Jews, who are part of the same Abrahamic religious tradition. A wife in these circumstances will convert to Islam if she wishes to live in the UAE.

In the event of a marital breakdown, it will be assumed as a matter of course that the children will be assigned to the care of the father. When the couple has been living in a country that does not follow Shariah (religious) law, on breakdown of the marriage, there are reports of children being kidnapped by the father. In these cases, the UAE's Shariah law supports the father, which can make access to children very problematic for the mother.

INSHA'ALLAH

Insha'allah is one of the most commonly heard phrases throughout the Arab world. It means "If God wills," and is used on any occasion when the future is concerned. To the Muslim mind, everything that happens is in the hands of God (Allah), so it would be presumptuous to claim that what will happen depends principally on someone's own efforts. It may sound as if *Insha'allah* is used to indicate that something will only happen if God takes a direct interest in doing it. However, this is not the case. It means instead that the individual will seek to perform whatever commitment has been made, but it must be borne in mind that God might have other plans.

In recent times, the word has come to take on a new, and more negative meaning, associated with second-hand procrastination, i.e. never getting things done for other people. *Insha'allah* is often heard for example in the classroom when homework is handed out. "*Insha'allah*, it will be done," the students will say—much to the frustration of the teacher, who might then hold little hope of seeing the work completed.

BACKHAND ECONOMY

Many large business deals are conducted in an opaque fashion, especially those related to defense and security. Rumors often circulate about whether under-the-table payments may have influenced a deal. Such rumors are often fed by poor information about the decision-making processes. This lack of transparency, combined with the patronage culture in which one individual takes care of the interests of his extended family, suffuses the UAE's business culture. People wish to protect the interests of their families and connections, and decisions are made that cannot be easily explained to outsiders.

WASTA

Wasta is an Arabic word meaning something like "influence," "favoritism" or "connections." It is a concept relating to the degree of connectedness that an individual may have with other people and organizations and, hence, the ability of that individual to get things done. It is not what you know but who you know that counts. In common with people of many other societies, Emiratis prefer to do business with people whom they know and trust. Since the process of getting to trust another person can be time-consuming and even expensive, it is more efficient to short-circuit this process by pointing to a connection with someone that can act as a symbol of trust and friendship.

Membership of the same family or tribe is perhaps the most powerful symbol of this instant connection; one Emirati introduced to another family member will immediately understand that the long years of established relationships mean the individual can be trusted, since their actions are guaranteed by elder members of the family. Nevertheless, trust can be lost in severe circumstances. In large households, powerful taboos can develop to ensure domestic harmony.

While the reasons behind *wasta* are understandable, in reality, those with *wasta* are often given privileged access to scarce resources that others cannot have —including the time and attention of important people and officials. Consequently, the *wasta*-holders get their business attended to more swiftly. Some people base their career on their possession of *wasta* and their ability, therefore, to complete paperwork and have decisions approved. Prospective business people will therefore customarily seek to equip themselves with allies with high levels of *wasta*.

Many foreign residents come to realize that the more *wasta* an Emirati has, the less likely they are to be blamed by police in a driving incident. At college, some students put little effort into their work, believing their *wasta*, based on family connections, will get them a prestigious government job, regardless of their grades. The engrained usage of *wasta* in Emirati society was popularized in the Emirati comedy film "Abood Kandaishan" (2014), by Fadel Al Mheiri, in which the protagonist tries to use his *wasta* to avoid being transferred from rural government control room where he has worked for thirteen years, to the big city of Abu Dhabi.

But times are changing. With professionalism more engrained into recruitment procedures, and with less government jobs to go around, *wasta* has less influence in Emirati society that it once had.

TOLERANCE AND PREJUDICE

At social gatherings conversations about religion and politics and, in particular Israel and Iran, are best avoided. Although there are plenty of far-sighted Emiratis with a mature appreciation of global politics, there are plenty more who hold prejudices that may lead to inflammatory arguments. Emiratis are passionately patriotic, and while some are willing to openly criticize the pace of development that has been embraced in the UAE, or the westernization of their youth, they would never put the blame for any social problems onto their much-respected leaders.

SENSE OF HUMOR

For Emiratis, sharing *nuktah*, which means a joke, is a part of everyday life. But social conservatism in the UAE means that there are many culture practises that are off-limits for humor, and these are areas that provide significant material for humor and satire in Western countries. Making a joke about someone while making them "lose face" is not acceptable and crosses the line of respect and that of any friendship.

Jokes require more than translation to be understood, so translating Western jokes to Arabic might not get the desired reaction. Emirati humor therefore often concentrates on stereotypes or physical comedy. More recently, social media has given Emiratis a platform for sharing their humor. On Youtube, Emiratis love to watch the new breed of young male Saudi stand-up comedy stars. On Instagram, the Emirati Abdullaziz Baz (@bin_baz) has 4.5 million followers checking in to see his slapstick pranks. Comedy provides young Gulf Arabs with a chance to show a lighter, warmer side to their culture. These youngsters are often painfully aware of the negative way in which Gulf Arabs are often portrayed in the Western media (as radical preachers or flashy billionaires) and are keen to present an alternative narrative of their culture.

chapter three

CUSTOMS & TRADITIONS

Customs and traditions are very important to Emiratis, perhaps even more so because of the comparatively short period in which they have been catapulted into the modern age. But feasting and celebration in the past, even a generation ago, was quite different from the lavish buffet spreads enjoyed today. Materialism has become a central part of celebrations as people wish to demonstrate their generosity and treat their friends and family to the good things of the world. Of course, not everyone is enamored of this change and many, especially the elderly and more spiritually concerned, feel that the real message of these celebrations is being compromised. Behind closed doors, some Emiratis also express frustration at the erosion of their Emirati identity and the feeling they are being engulfed by a wave of Western cultural values, adopting a culture of "shop-till-you-drop" consumerism and "Friday Brunches' (the extravagant afternoon buffets served at hotels, often accompanied by free-flowing alcohol, that are popular with Western expatriates).

A number of old Emirati traditions have been transformed and even reinvented for the modern age. Falconry and horsemanship, for example, were skills necessary for survival in a difficult environment, but have now become rather glamorous celebrations of a semi-mythical past rather different from the reality. It is quite common for societies to re-create their past so that it appears to be rather more convivial than it might really have been. For a visitor to the UAE, therefore, when it is possible to gain access to the performance of tradition, care should be taken to try to appreciate the original contours of the event.

FALCONRY

Falconry has been an integral part of Bedouin life for centuries, so much so that the emblem of the UAE consists of a golden falcon with a disc in the middle, showing the UAE flag and seven stars representing the seven Emirates. The falcon as a totemic symbol represents force, speed, and courage, and is the inspiration behind some of the UAE's iconic futuristic architecture, such as the UAE National Pavilion in the Dubai World Expo 2020, which takes the shape of a falcon's wing feathers.

The sharp-eyed birds of prey can see potential victims from an enormous distance away and have proved themselves to be useful and valuable companions in the desert, as they can be trained

to deliver their prey without killing it first. Sheikh
Zayed developed a deep passion for falconry, which
has helped the practice to flourish. It is still quite
common for young Emirati men to keep a pet
falcon in their homes, training them to retrieve
targets flung into the far distance and to return
to their arms. Falcon's heads are usually covered
with a leather hood, which is an essential aspect of
training. Visitors can learn more about falconry at
the Abu Dhabi Falcon Hospital, which is the largest
falcon hospital in the world.

CALENDARS
The UAE follows the standard Islamic calendar,
although most official documents are dated using

both the Islamic and Western systems. The Islamic calendar is based on the lunar cycle with twelve such months in each year, amounting to about 354 days per year. The first year of the calendar is marked by the *Hijra*, in which the Prophet Mohammed traveled from Mecca to Medina. This occurred, in the Western calendar, in the year 570. So the year 2018, according to the Islamic calendar, is 1439 –1440 AH (After the *Hijra*).

In the UAE, Friday and Saturday are the weekend days off and most retail outlets and tourist attractions are closed on Friday mornings. The differing weekends causes some difficulties for organizations headquartered in a Western country, as the only days people from both countries are scheduled to work are from Monday to Thursday. When situations require urgent attention, some staff must work long hours to catch up with overseas colleagues working different time zones and days.

As Friday is considered the holiest day, it is quite common for Muslim men to attend mosque on Friday morning or lunchtime, in order to listen to a sermon from a favored imam. In other countries, such a sermon can be the starting point for a political demonstration, but this has not been the case in the UAE, partially because the contents are monitored by the authorities. The mosques' loudspeakers broadcast Friday sermons outdoors, so if the mosque is full, those standing outside can still hear what's being said.

HOLIDAYS

It can be difficult to make holiday plans because the exact dates that religious public holidays fall are not declared until just a few days beforehand, when prices shoot up and flights book up quickly. As well as a dozen or so religious public holidays, residents also get at least one day off work to mark National Day on December 2, which commemorates the unification of the Emirates in 1971. Some Emiratis mark this joyous occasion by decking out their cars with foil artwork depicting the UAE's leaders and flag, and showing their vehicle off in a jovial car parade which involves the prolonged tooting of car horns and spraying party string over each other. Another patriotic holiday introduced to the UAE calendar in 2015 is "Commemoration Day," when the sacrifices of Emirati martyrs are remembered. Tributes are paid to those who died in civil, humanitarian, and military service.

RAMADAN

Ramadan is one of the most important times of the year for Muslims, when a month of fasting during daylight hours culminates in the feast of Eid Al-Fitr. The UAE's hotels lay on sumptuous *iftar* (fast-breaking) buffets over Ramadan, which are a popular way for non-Muslims to join in the festivities.

Fasting has the benefits of concentrating the mind on the spiritual sphere, as well as promoting

self-discipline. During this time, which occupies
the ninth month of the lunar calendar, Muslims
refrain from drinking, eating, smoking, or any kind
of sexual activity during daylight hours. Emiratis
spend their evenings feasting with families and
friends, taking turns to entertain each other.

Ramadan has a strong impact upon working
life, since hours of work may be adjusted to reduce
stress for those fasting. In any case, many people
feel drained during the day and, consequently, their
level of work and judgment may dip. Small children,
pregnant or breastfeeding women, and those with
medical conditions such as diabetes may waive the
obligation to fast. Children are usually permitted
to stay awake until late to enjoy the celebrations,
which can make them fractious during the day.
Many spend their daylight hours praying, reading
the Koran, and snoozing. Specially made Ramadan
TV dramas are watched by millions across the Arab
world, and in recent years, these have explored
controversial political issues.

Non-Muslims are advised that during Ramadan,
they cannot eat, drink or smoke in public during
daylight hours, even taking a sip of water in the
comfort of their car (although feeding children in
public is acceptable.) Those who drive just before
sunset are warned to be cautious of the alertness
of other drivers. A handful of café and restaurants
in each city are permitted to stay open during
daylight hours over Ramadan for the benefit of
non-Muslims, so long as they black out their doors

and windows. In multinational organizations, water dispensers and coffee machines are removed from sight, and most employers will provide closed rooms where non-Muslims can eat without calling attention to themselves.

EID AL-FITR

This festival, which marks the end of Ramadan, is the largest and most important festival in the UAE. The streets of the UAE are lit up with twinkling Eid lights, as over the course of several days, Emiratis organize extensive feasts to entertain family and friends, assembling traditional meals of barbecued lambs and large dishes of pilaf rice. It is recommended to bless your Emirati acquaintances with *Eid Mubarak* during this period, which translates as "Happy Eid."

Traditionally, Emirati women clean their homes and decorate themselves with henna and traditional perfumes. Children collect money from relatives in the neighborhood, chanting a phrase from Emirati folklore meaning "We have been given Eidiya." Whereas this tradition used to involve small coins or sweets, nowadays it tends to be banknotes, and stores do a roaring trade in "Eid gifts."

OTHER RELIGIOUS HOLIDAYS

Emiratis also celebrate the holiday of Eid al-Adha, known as the festival of sacrifice, when Muslims recall the sacrifices made by Abraham. He was asked by God to sacrifice his own son, although once he'd demonstrated his obedience, God provided a substitute in the form of a ram. People sacrifice an animal on this day, generally a lamb, which is then used as the basis of the feast. Customarily, a third of the meat of the animal is eaten by those present, a third is given away to friends, and the remaining third is donated to the poor.

Two other holy days are the Mouloud, commemorating the birth of the Prophet Mohammed, and the Leilat al-Meiraj, his ascension into heaven upon reaching spiritual perfection.

Given that people from around the world work in the UAE, nearly every religious festival is celebrated in some form. Work schedules aren't usually changed to cater to them—Christmas Day, for example, is usually a regular working day. But many of the less obviously religious Christmas traditions can be publicly enjoyed in the UAE by everyone—grandiose Christmas trees fill hotel lobbies, and supermarkets are stocked up with festive foods. Similarly, Diwali, which is the Hindu festival of lights, is celebrated with fireworks, light spectacles, and traditional dancing.

NEW YEAR

There are two New Year celebrations in the UAE—the start of the Islamic New Year, which varies according to the sighting of the moon, and the Western New Year on January 1. The Islamic New Year is spent with family or in prayer and contemplation, and people are increasingly using the day to make resolutions.

OTHER CELEBRATIONS

Family occasions such as marriages and birthdays are opportunities to reaffirm social relationships as well as occasions to celebrate.

Informal celebrations are also likely to break out in response to important sporting, social, or political events. Winning a big football game, for example, inspires a procession of beeping cars, with riders leaning out of windows waving scarves. On occasions of spontaneous celebration, those with access to Emirati women's quarters may hear the famous ululation (a high-pitched, celebratory trilling vocal sound)

Funerals tend to be low-key and the deceased is, according to tradition, buried secretly in the desert wrapped in a simple white sheet. Funerals are not usually the occasion for the mass public gathering of relatives and friends found in other Middle Eastern societies, except on the occasion of the death of a sheikh. When Sheikh Zayed died, forty days of national mourning was declared, with government departments closing for eight days and private companies for three.

LOCAL CUSTOMS AND FOLKLORE

The two great traditions of Emirati society— the desert and the sea—have both inspired many legends, told and retold around campfires for generations. Common heroes include the men so generous that they sold their last few possessions to feed their guests, those who suffer the slings and arrows of fortune, like Aladdin, or the servant who is also the leader: this is a person who seems to hold a lowly position but whose wisdom and streetwise ability can guide rulers on to the desired path, offering the opportunity for glory even to the poorest individual.

Folk wisdom in the UAE dates from the pre-Islamic period, and therefore is occasionally frowned upon when it appears to contradict Islamic beliefs. Many Emiratis particularly in rural areas still believe in the existence of *djinn,* which are folklore spirits that can be

either good or bad, and can take the form of people we know.

The myth of *djinn* was immortalized on the big screen in the Hollywood movie of the same name (2013), which was filmed in Ras Al Khaimah. It was loosely based on the legend of Umm al Duwais, a murderous *djinn* temptress who according to one story had donkey hooves as feet and the eyes of a cat. For hundreds of years, such stories were recounted from one generation to the next but because so few were ever written down, many have been lost to the sands of time.

Because of the UAE's coastal position and location on various trade routes, traditions from other cultures have been absorbed into Emirati heritage. Ancient Mesopotamian influences in pottery making, for example, can be seen in archaeological finds. Over the centuries, distinctive forms of cultural expression have been brought into being, including boat building, the use of folk medicine, and the creation of poetry to express ideas that are characteristically Emirati in nature. The late Sheikh Zayed observed that a country that did not know its past had neither a present nor future. Maintaining knowledge and appreciation of the past, and allowing this to guide development of society in the future, is an important charge that Sheikh Zayed laid upon his government.

Numerous museums exist to inform tourists about Emirati heritage, but for the people themselves, traditional culture is kept alive at family social gatherings and through annual heritage festivals. At the Al Dhafra Festival in Madinat Zayed, thousands flock from as far afield as Saudi Arabia for the camel beauty contests, and at the Sheikh Zayed Heritage Festival in Al Wathba, folk heritage is celebrated through traditional dancing and food. Both festivals take place in Abu Dhabi Emirate in December.

The smaller Emirates have retained more of a nostalgia for the past than the high-rise cities of Abu Dhabi and Dubai, and local heritage can be better appreciated by visiting the well-preserved forts and souks in Al Ain, and the heritage district in Sharjah.

Emirati Poetry

Writing poetry is one of the most noble activities in which an Emirati man can engage. Bedouin poetry, which is known as Nabati, ranks alongside falconry in demonstrating manliness, sensitivity, and understanding of one's cultural heritage. Neighboring Iran has, for centuries, had a tradition of epic poetry, which has perhaps helped the Bedouin spinning of tales around the campfire to become elevated into a high form of art. It would not be seemly to dwell on romantic love (and some of those who have done so have been jailed for breaching public morality), and Nabati poets try instead to reflect on their place in the universe and on matters of spirituality.

Traditional poetry is experiencing something of a resurgence in the region. Universities across the UAE also hold annual talent contests, in which the most popular contestants are almost always the poets. And millions of people from across the Middle East turn on their televisions to watch reality poetry contests, such as "Prince of Poets" and "Million's Poets," both of which are filmed in Abu Dhabi and based on the same formula as regional pop singing contests "Arabs Got Talent." The prizes are worth millions of dollars, and the show also acts as a way for young Arabs to voice their feelings on contemporary issues.

In the desert communities, *Al shellah* is a form of chanting without the accompaniment of an instrument. It is practiced throughout the Arab Gulf, with variations from one country to another. The UAE's *shellah* is mostly composed by famous Emirati poets and can be about any subject: praising the beauty of a camel, sailing, or hunting, for instance. In the past, people used to chant *shellah* to pass time: during desert crossings, when setting sail or, at night, around campfires; a good *shellah* is not just about the poetry, but also the interpretation, the vocal intonation, and how rhythmic the chanting is.

While *shellah* has been gradually forgotten over the last few decades, it has always been present at the Al Dhafra Festival, an annual heritage festival and camel beauty pageant that take place in Abu Dhabi's Empty Quarter desert. During camel beauty competitions, there is a long wait for winners to be announced, which is almost always passed with outbursts of *shellah*, chanted loudly by a camel owner in the audience.

This distinctive dance is very different to the forms of dance commonly served up to tourists, such as belly dancing that takes place on desert safaris, or the Arabic entertainment that performed in the lobbies or restaurants of hotels. But visitors lucky enough to catch a heritage festival during their stay can get a chance to see more authentic Emirati cultural performances. The sight of rifles can cause some alarm to onlookers, and it is also customary during Emirati wedding parties for the rifles to be fired loudly into the air. But rest assured that no ill feeling is intended.

Musical instruments that are traditionally played by Emiratis include the *oud* (a stringed instrument played all over the Arab world), drums, tambourine (which Emiratis call the *daf*), *rababa* (a stringed instrument), and the *doumbek* [a goblet-shaped drum].

Another aspect of Emirati music, now almost extinct, are the songs of the Gulf Arab pearl divers. This singing, which played a key role psychologically for those men undertaking such a dangerous job, was explored and documented in the film "A Grain of Sand" (2017), by British musician Jason Carter.

TRADITIONAL EMIRATI DANCING

Emirati dance is performed to mark the bringing together of two different tribes or families, which happens on special occasion such as Eid, engagements, and wedding parties. The most popular form of dance is the Al Ayyala (or 'Yola'), which is practiced in north-western Oman as well as the UAE. Male dancers in white *kandoras* (traditional long male robe) chant poetry to the rhythmic, trance-like beat of drums, as a battle scene is simulated through dance. Two rows of about twenty men face each other, carrying thin bamboo sticks to signify spears and swords. Between the rows, musicians play drums, tambourines, and brass cymbals. The rows of men move their heads and sticks synchronously with the rhythm of the drum, and other performers move around the rows holding swords or rifles, which they throw into the sky and catch. Young girls, wearing colorful traditional dresses, stand at the front, tossing their long hair from side to side.

chapter four

MAKING FRIENDS

Friendship in the Emirati community is almost wholly regulated along gender lines, and there are few circumstances in which a man and a woman can be friends without provoking a scandal.

Religious, historical, and managerial implications mean that establishing a genuine relationship with an Emirati on an equal basis is unlikely. Working together in an organization is probably the most common way of creating a level of trust. Expatriates with similar cultural backgrounds to Emiratis find it easier to initiate relationships, and Muslim expatriates might feel they are part of a larger Muslim community in which all are more or less equal in the face of God. Those of Arab descent also have the advantage of being able to converse with Emiratis in Arabic.

Friendship is taken very seriously by Emiratis, and it represents a serious commitment in terms of time and honesty. Once a relationship is established, it can hardly ever be reversed (which makes enmities very severe). Some Emiratis have become disenchanted with visitors who seem at first to be

open and friendly—which would demonstrate
a definite commitment to friendship—but who
then seem to back off.

ATTITUDES TOWARD FOREIGNERS

Emiratis are very hospitable and welcoming, but
also prone to ascribing certain characteristics
to foreigners based on their nationality, without
intending to be insulting. People with white skin
often receive more respectful treatment than
those with darker skin when first encountered.
However, the UAE is rapidly becoming a
cosmopolitan society. Residents often have
considerable experience of world cultures, which
is leading to greater tolerance and understanding.
There is a distinct multinational expatriate culture
that is emerging too, particularly in Dubai in
which friendships are being formed based not so
much on nationality but on shared interests.

GREETINGS

Emirati friends and family of the same gender
often greet each other with a nose kiss, by rubbing
noses with each other, but it would be considered
strange and perhaps amusing if a foreign visitor
tried to do the same.

Even though Emiratis are almost always very
used to conversing in English, It is always much
appreciated when a foreigner tries to make a

greeting in Arabic. The Arabic language is used
in a formal way in many situations. The Arabic
greeting universally employed, "*Salaam Aleikum*,"
has the sense of "May peace be with you," and
the proper response is very similar, "*Wa Aleikum
as-Salaam*." This is used face-to-face as well as on
the telephone and in e-mails. Arabic speakers will,
depending on the circumstances, go on to exchange
semi-ritualized pleasantries for some time: "How
are you?" "How is your health, your family?"
The proper Arabic response to these questions
is "*Al-Hamdu Lillah*" (this varies slightly with
dialects), which may be translated as "Thanks be to
God." Conversation is another opportunity for the
individual to demonstrate their submission to God.
Depending on the situation, there may also be offers
of hospitality, and refreshments. It is generally polite
to accept something when it is offered to give the
other person the opportunity to demonstrate their
hospitality.

In formal written communications or public
addresses to organizations owned, or largely
managed, by Muslim people, it is customary to
begin with the religious invocation that means "In
the Name of God the Compassionate, the Merciful."
Visitors are advised to seek advice from Emiratis
in this regard or to pay attention to examples in
newspapers and brochures, as to the phrasing
required. Also bear in mind to be very discreet
when using any kind of illustration or graphic with
a communication.

HOSPITALITY

Hospitality is one of the central virtues of Arab society. Its importance derives not just from an innate sense of decency, but from the historical background of life in the desert. In order for trade to flourish over long distances, it was vital that travelers could be sure that they would receive a safe and hearty welcome when away from home. This has become thoroughly integrated into Emirati society, and all members will take whatever opportunity they can to host other people with whatever might be available. What has changed in recent decades is the amount of money that most people are able to deploy and, hence, the scale of hospitality on offer.

Occasionally it might appear that people are competing with each other to demonstrate their virtue by offering ever more lavish refreshments. If enjoying the generosity of one person, it is nearly always a bad idea to comment on hospitality received elsewhere, especially if the current hospitality appears to be inferior in some way.

When accepting an invitation, it is as well to be aware that social occasions often last until the early hours of the morning. You should be prepared to spend this time, or politely make it known that you can only attend a portion of the event. Unexpectedly leaving early is likely to be interpreted as an expression of dissatisfaction, which would reflect poorly on the host's sense of hospitality. On the other hand, be sensitive to a dropping off of conversation after a meal is finished as a signal that it is time to go.

In the past, guests would belch to demonstrate they are replete, but this custom appears to have died out and is certainly not recommended! Guests should be fulsome and genuine in gratitude to the host, who will accept compliments gracefully.

INVITATIONS HOME

Invitations to the home of an Emirati person are rare and valuable opportunities to get to know somebody. Being invited to a large compound with an extended family is quite different from being invited to the apartment of a young man or a couple, but in any case, it is appropriate to bring a small gift but don't take anything that might be seen as a slight on the hospitality that the host might provide. Don't take food, and especially don't take alcohol.

It is normal to take off shoes when entering someone else's house and to sit on cushions or low stools, and this requires some consideration of how to sit. Practice sitting cross-legged, keeping your legs covered. Women are advised to wear loose-fitting trousers, if not an *abaya*, to ensure modesty. In an all-female home environment, Emirati women may feel comfortable to take off their headscarves, and in doing it sometimes feels to a non-Muslim visitor as though social barriers also come down.

Depending on the type of social event concerned, there may be a fair amount of sitting down and not doing very much. This may appear unproductive, but it is an important part of getting to know each other and feeling trust in each other's presence. If men and women jointly visit a house, they will be unlikely to meet inside until it is time for them to leave, as men and women are strictly segregated. Women tend to spend time dressing and beautifying each other, but this varies a great deal. Emirati women are usually forthcoming in remarking whether or not they like a particular item of clothing or hairstyle, or point out that someone has gained or lost weight, but no offence is probably intended in such remarks.

Strong, bitter shots of Arabic coffee and dates are likely to be served regularly, as they have been for centuries. One can imagine how the sweet dates and strong coffee would provide the perfect burst of energy needed, after spending time in the desert sun. It would be impolite to refuse too much of what is offered so, even if an individual maintains strict dietary habits, they should still accept what they can. Vegetarianism is not really part of Arabic culture, but suitable side dishes are likely to available such as bread, hummus, yogurt, lentils, and rice dishes. The syrupy Turkish sweet *baklava* and Emirati sweet fried dumplings *luqaimat* are both delicious deserts traditionally enjoyed in Emirati homes.

MANNERS

In both Arabic and Islamic custom, it is common for the left-hand side of the body to be considered impure and belonging to the devil. Consequently, items should be handed to another person only using the right hand, and this should also be used to receive items. When receiving something from a person with high status, the left hand may be placed underneath the right hand or supporting the wrist, but never in contact with the hand of the person giving something. Emiratis occasionally break this taboo by grasping a trusted person with two hands. In no circumstances should the left hand be used when eating communally, or when taking food from a bowl that other people are also using. Most Emiratis prefer to eat with their hands when they're at home. Emirati children are required to write with their right hands irrespective of their natural proclivity, as is the case in many Asian countries, and this sometimes hampers them in their studies. However, comments about this would be considered impolite.

Muslim people are expected to wash their hands and arms up to the elbows, and feet and legs up to the knees prior to praying. Anything to do with the feet is likely to be considered unclean, and care should be taken not to point the feet at anyone or to expose the soles of the feet carelessly. Further, there is a correlation between status and being highest in the air, even when sitting cross-legged, and care should be taken to ensure not to tower over people who are seated. Following the examples of others will provide clues to the right behavior.

Finally, it is considered polite to efface oneself in many social situations—by persuading another person to go through the door first, for example, or by ordering a meal in a restaurant. This, like paying the bill for a group meal, can be quite an intense social struggle. Visitors should put up a little opposition before giving way gracefully, thereby permitting the other person to gain status by demonstrating generosity of spirit. It is necessary to refuse something several times before convincing another person the item is definitely not wanted. Do not offer an Emirati person something just once and accept the first, ritualized refusal. Make the same offer at least twice, remembering that Emiratis prize generosity above almost any other virtue.

chapter five

THE EMIRATIS AT HOME

THE HOUSEHOLD

The UAE's heritage and traditions are very much alive and well today, but to find them you must look beyond the skyscrapers and malls and head into the Emirati home. In Western society, parents pride themselves on raising their children to be independent and to live away from them when they reach adulthood. Conversely, in the Arab world, group identity and sense of belonging are fundamental. Emirati parents require that their children live at home until they are married, and then may even encourage their son or daughter to bring their new spouse to live with them—or at least next door.

Well-established Emirati families tend to live in large, central houses or with extended family in a compound of buildings. Privacy is paramount and homes are customarily surrounded by high walls to stop anyone looking in. Unexpected guests are frowned upon, so it is better to wait for a specific appointment. While affluent Westerners living in the UAE prefer to have villas with pools, swimming is not a popular pastime among Emirati citizens, who might instead have a traditional tent erected in their yard. Outdoor garden space isn't highly prized, as Emiratis prefer to spend time in the shade or indoors, often with the blinds drawn. For this reason, the UAE has one of the highest rates of vitamin D deficiency in the world (over 85 percent, according to a 2016 study).

Since men and women are not generally permitted to occupy the same space, parallel facilities and rooms are built to enable men to have their own dining rooms, seating areas, and bathrooms, and women the same, depending on resources available. Children up to the age of seven are generally exempt from this restriction, and girls are introduced into segregation on their eighth birthday.

FAMILY LIFE

In the 1970s, it was common for Emirati families to have at least seven children. Today the average is about three, as Emiratis are tending to marry later in life. Nevertheless, this average still means that households tend to be large and busy. In the case of husbands with multiple wives, each is expected to have her own household within the larger compound and, should one have a new maid or driver, the others must receive the same. The relationships between the wives and their various children and relatives can vary considerably. The first wife is almost always Emirati, and subsequent wives are sometimes foreign. Incoming women and any accompanying family members will bring their own customs and tastes, which lend some variety to the ways in which children are raised. It is often the case that the first wife is welcomed into the fold by extended family members, and it is she who is invited to social gatherings, rather than subsequent wives and their children.

CHILDHOOD

These days, Emirati children tend to live privileged lives. The concept of "spoiling" children is still a relatively foreign concept. After all, up until only fifty years ago, limited household income meant it was nearly impossible to spoil children with too many material possessions. There is also a tendency for children to be over reliant on maids, who might not have confidence or authority to discipline them. The maids are inclined to indulge children's whims, hand out sugary treats on demand, and allow them to play video games unrestricted. These potential pitfalls are not confined to the Emirati population—plenty of expatriate parents encounter similar issues. But the issue is exacerbated in Emirati households because parents usually employ one maid per child, rather than one per family. It is not unusual for parents to have up to seven children, each with maids, plus at least one driver, all living in the same household. All this attentiveness means children can easily become overindulged.

The UAE is a safe country, and Emirati parents are usually happy to let their children play outside from a young age. Anyone driving through Emirati neighborhoods at night should keep a watchful eye out for children on the roads. Bedtime for children in

Emirati culture is less strictly enforced than it is in the West.

While Western expatriate families might try to make the most of the sunshine during the day, Emiratis tend to stay indoors—a natural inclination, given that for their ancestors, shelter from the sun was essential to survival. They therefore tend to go to sleep much later, in order to make the most of the twilight hours. Nowhere is this more noticeable than in the UAE's parks. Mornings and early afternoons are when the Westerners come out to play, as they tend to bed their children first. The Levantine Arabs come afterwards, followed in the evenings by the Emiratis, whose children will often take afternoon naps to catch up on sleep.

EDUCATION

In the past, the Bedouin did not write things down, relying instead on an oral tradition to pass on the songs and stories of the great deeds of their forefathers. In his book *Sand Huts and Salty Water*, Abu Dhabi's first schoolteacher, Ahmed Mansour M. Khateeb, describes teaching the first generation of Emirati schoolboys from the capital to read and write in the late 1950s. In recent years, the leadership has been actively encouraging its people to read, with annual book and literature festivals held in Sharjah, Abu Dhabi, and Dubai. New libraries have opened across the county, and 2016 was declared "the year of reading."

Most teachers come from overseas, and attempts made in recent years to lure more Emiratis into the teaching profession have so far been met with limited success.

Schools are generally well resourced, but teachers customarily rely for their livelihood on not upsetting the students, some of whom learn to play on this.

Long family vacations overseas are common. This leads to a broadening of experience, but as most Emirati families pull their children out of school in early June for a three month-long summer break, their schooling suffers as a result.

Until recently, the education system has been dominated by the rote learning approach, in which students learn by heart what teachers prescribe for them and are rewarded for repeating it verbatim. Children are also encouraged to memorize and recite the Koran as part of their education. This has changed somewhat in recent years as more creative

approaches to education have been introduced. Maths and science are now taught in English, somewhat controversially. While Emiratis tend to be proficient in speaking English, many children struggle to write it, and there is also concern that their standard of written Arabic is faltering too. While in the past, Emirati children graduated from high school expecting a lucrative government job to fall into their laps, the government is now keen to impress on them that this is no longer a guarantee. Current leaders recognize that this young generation is vital to in shaping the new knowledge-based economy.

Engineering is a career held in high esteem by Emiratis, and young Emirati boys are often encouraged by their parents to pursue either engineering or business-related subjects at university. Emirati girls are now educated up to college level, and while the range of topics that they're permitted to study has expanded, the head of the family can wield a veto in the case of debate.

DAILY LIFE
Daily routine is punctuated by the five daily calls to prayer. Since Emiratis often live in suburbs on the very outskirts of town, much of their routine involves driving (or being driven) from air-conditioned cars to air-conditioned homes, or offices, and back. People often dress for a much cooler climate than that of the UAE, because they

spend their whole time in an artificially cool environment.

In the past, women's domestic work involved trips to the souk, together with food preparation and housework. Much of this has been eased by labor-saving devices and domestic help, with Emirati women supervising domestic arrangements so that they comply with their standards.

Domestic Help

Cultural attitudes toward domestic workers are shaped by the fact that slavery endured in the Gulf much later than in other parts of the world. According to Matthew Hopper in his book *Slaves of One Master: Globalization and Slavery in Arabia in the age of Empire,* up to 800,000 slaves were transported to the Gulf in the latter half of the nineteenth century, the vast majority of whom came from East Africa. When the pearl and date markets collapsed with the global recession in the 1930s, many slaves were freed, and the UAE is now home to a sizeable proportion of black Emirati families who are the descendants of those slaves. Slavery was finally abolished by law in 1963, but until recently, the UAE's domestic helpers, who, these days, commonly come from the Philippines, Indonesia, Sri Lanka, and Nepal, still faced limited protection from unscrupulous employers. In 2017, this changed when a law was enacted giving domestic staff a weekly day off, thirty days of paid annual leave, the right to retain their passport, and

at least twelve hours of rest each day. It is hoped
that this law will stamp out cases of mistreatment,
which persist in a minority of Emirati households.

CLOTHES
Women
Young Emirati women still conform to their
societal norms by wearing black *abayas* to cover
their bodies and *shaylas* over their heads. But this
traditional dress has been adapted over the years to
offer women avenues to express their own sense of
style. Their choice of fabrics, the decoration on the
hemlines, and the shoes they wear are opportunities
to establish their
individuality. Aspects of
style that can be publicly
displayed tend to be
accentuated, and many
young Emirati women
indulge themselves with
the highest, flashiest
heels that money can
buy, as well as stylish
designer handbags, a
heavily made-up face,
and beautifully elaborate
nail art. The market for
accessories is booming
in the UAE. Unlike
their more conservative

neighbors, the Saudi, some young ladies wear their *shayla* so their hair is exposed at the front. Many also wear their *abayas* in a way that exposes flashes of colorful garments underneath. More conservative women wear their *abayas* closed and a veil or *burqa* (mask) covering their faces, and underneath they wear a *mukhawwar*, which is a traditional long dress with embroidery on the chest and wrists. Emirati women visit a tailor to choose the material they like, and the *mukhawwar* and the *abaya* are cut to fit. This is usually performed by Pakistani men who are renown for their sewing skills.

Misunderstandings prevail in the West over the choice Muslim women make to wear the *abaya*. Historically, it was simply a light robe used to cover the body—a practical necessity in the desert sun—but not all tribes saw it as an essential piece of clothing. These days, in a country with such a large foreign population, the black *abaya* communicates societal status as a Gulf Arab woman, as well as signifying religious and cultural values. The Koran is somewhat vague about how exactly women should cover themselves, leaving much to interpretation, and Islamic fashion is constantly pushing the boundaries in terms of style, cut, and color.

HENNA

For festive occasions, women customarily decorate their hands and feet with henna, a brown paste derived from the henna plant, which has the

THE BURQA

Visitors to the UAE might notice older Emirati women wearing a metallic-yellow face mask. This mask, known as the *burqa*, is traditionally worn by women across the Gulf, but in each region it has taken on a slightly different shape and style. In Dubai the *burqa* has a narrow top and broad, curved bottom; in Al Ain, the design features a narrow top and bottom. While the reason behind wearing the mask are to do with protecting a woman's modesty, the *burqa* is also reputed to have a beautifying and whitening effect on the skin. Women who have worn the mask all their lives claim to have milky-white skin and fewer wrinkles in the area where they have worn the mask, because it shields those areas from the sun's glare. The *burqa* also conveniently hides wrinkles, scars, and broken teeth. These days, the *burqa* has been revived as a symbol of Emirati culture because of an extremely popular television animation with Emirati children, called "Freej." It's about four Emirati *burqa*-wearing old women who live in a secluded Dubai neighborhood, trying to cope with the city's rapid modernization.

particular property of adhering to the skin and remaining there. While in the past, a designated older Emirati woman applied the henna to the women and girls of her tribe, today, the females tend to visit salons where specialists from other parts of the Middle East apply the designs. Left to dry, the intricate swirling patterns of the dye darken, turning from a brown outline to a vivid red-brown after a couple of days.

Henna is a significant part of an Emirati woman's wedding preparations, with the bride's female relatives and friends hosting a henna night three days before the big event. The designs are believed to contain *barakah*, an unseen flow of positive energy from Allah that brings blessings to the wearer and protects against evil spirits.

Men

Emirati men are among the smartest-looking
in the world with their immaculately trimmed
beards and long, crisp and spotlessly white
kanduras (gowns). At first sight, the Emirati
kandura might appear the same as the Saudi,
Kuwaiti, Qatari, and Omani traditional garments,
but in fact they all differ slightly. The Emirati
kandura is distinguished by the fact it tends not
to have a collar, and usually has a long loose tassel
with matching embroidery along the neckline
and on the sleeves. These days, some fashionable
Emirati men might distinguish themselves from

the crowd by wearing a blue, brown, or black *kandura,* but they remain a minority.

On their heads, the men tend to wear the *ghutrah.* It is a square cloth, usually made of cotton, either in plain white or red with white embroidery. Young Emirati men sometimes prefer to wear baseball hats for more relaxed occasions, or may even dare to go out with no head covering at all. You might also see a man wearing a dark cloak over the *kandura,* known as a *bisht,* which is worn by royalty or important figures on ceremonial occasions.

It would be a mistake to assume that an Emirati man in traditional dress doesn't embrace the modern world. Most are extremely well traveled, and enjoy watching the latest Hollywood and Bollywood movies, and listening to popular music on their latest Smartphones.

FAMILY OCCASIONS
Friday is a day for meeting with the extended family. This enables families to reaffirm relationships through feasting, giving gifts, and generally being together, although men and women do so separately. Family occasions will generally be held in the house, but it is also increasingly common for young people to meet in restaurants and cafes. Gatherings at home tend to center on the communal meal, but there

may also be singing and ululating in the women's section, and perhaps poetry recitations among the men. The modern world has impacted upon family occasions in the UAE as elsewhere with young people preferring to be messaging friends or playing online games. Negotiation and compromise are the order of the day.

Food at home
The food eaten in Emirati households has changed dramatically in the last fifty years, as the import of food from abroad has given the Emiratis a taste for international cuisine, particularly of the fast food variety. But at Friday family gatherings, traditional dishes are still enjoyed, especially Al Machboos, a blend of meat (usually mutton), rice, dried lime, saffron, and a medley of vegetables. In the past, fish was the staple diet, often served with rice and lime, and meat was regarded as a delicacy to be served on special occasions such as the birth of a baby, the event of someone managing to memorize the Koran, or the Sheikh paying a visit.

Today, the younger generation of Emirati women tend to demonstrate their culinary skills by putting traditional cooking aside in favor of baking cakes, often elaborately decorating them and posting pictures of them on Instagram. Meals are generally cooked by the domestic helper under supervision, or ordered in.

THE IMPORTANCE OF SCENT IN EMIRATI CULTURE

Visitors may well be curious about the rich, distinctively Arabian scent of *oud* in smoke that wafts from burners on perfume counters throughout the shopping malls. *Oud* comes in two basic forms—the resin-saturated wood, which is burnt for its rich-smelling smoke, and from distilled oil. Both forms originate from the wood of the agar tree which, if infected with a particular type of mold, produces a dark, scented resin.

In almost every Emirati home, *oud* in its wood form is burnt at least once a week, especially on Fridays, as a sign of hospitality to guests. As well as being burnt in the form of pieces of woodchip, *oud* comes in the form of *bukhoor*, a compressed, potent sawdust powder.

If you are invited to a gathering of women in an Emirati home, an *oud* burner will most likely be passed around the group, and the women will take it in turns breathe it in and waft the smoke under their *abayas* to absorb the rich scent into their clothes. This deeply sensual ritual is likely to be repeated throughout the evening.

Oud isn't just burnt at social gatherings. It's also an integral part of everyday life, as a way of getting rid of cooking smells and generally acting as an air freshener. The perfumes that are infused into the *oud* (which have sometimes been left to steep for as long as three months) have changed with the times, and some young Emiratis prefer a blend in which the sweeter notes of Western perfumes are added to the more traditional Arabian tones. Western luxury brands such as Gucci, Tom Ford, Dior, and Armani are targeting Arabian Gulf customers by including a touch of *oud* in their perfume collections. Pass any young Emirati woman and you are likely to be hit with the scent of perfume, as applying their signature perfume in liberal doses is a central aspect of their morning beauty regime.

Traditional scents that are still used today by the UAE's traditional perfume makers include amber, sandalwood, musk, and saffron. Also popular in perfume blends is frankincense, the resin extracted from the boswellia tree that is grown in neighboring Oman. In addition to its antiseptic benefit, some Emiratis still believe it has the power to cast out *djinn*.

Quality *oud* doesn't come cheap— a pound of *oud* can fetch US $20,000. One reason it is so expensive is its rarity; by some estimates, fewer than 2 percent of wild agar trees produce it. Experts claim that the very best *oud* comes from the oldest trees, which are even scarcer.

Applying an intoxicating perfume to both clothes and skin is an essential ritual that brides go through in preparation for their wedding, as perfume is considered to be an essential aphrodisiac in Emirati culture.

chapter six

TIME OUT

In countries with a hot climate there is often a culture of long periods of leisure time during the day. These hours are generally spent with people of the same gender, which influences the kinds of activity that take place. The time is spent relaxing and talking, and creating and confirming relationships. Today, new forms of technology have greatly expanded the kinds of leisure activity open to Emiratis, but cultural norms remain. Wanting to be alone, and the whole notion of individualism, is anathema to Emiratis, and solitary pursuits such as reading books have been slow to catch on.

SHOPPING

Vast areas are dedicated to retail space in the UAE—probably rather more than sustained demand really justifies, given the arrival of online shopping—and almost all the global designer brands have opened stores. Malls are sometimes themed to attract tourists, such as the Ibn Battuta Mall, with its decor reflecting parts of the world that the famous medieval, Arab explorer Ibn Battuta once visited.

Malls also offer expensive lotteries and giveaways to lure shoppers.

Bartering still takes place in the *souks*, which in Dubai go by the name of what they sell: "gold souk," "spice souk," "perfume souk," and "textile souk."

Arabic textiles and perfumes can make distinctive gifts. For made-in-the-UAE products, try Al Foah organic dates (from Al Ain), camel milk soap (from Dubai's camel soap factory) or Al Nassma camel chocolate (made in Abu Dhabi); these are available at most souvenir stores.

CULTURAL ACTIVITIES

Many important cultural artifacts are kept in private households, to be appreciated by their owners and his guests. But there are also a growing number of public spaces exhibiting items from the UAE's heritage.

Museums

Although the UAE has in the past been more associated with malls than museums, the country is now making a concerted effort to expand its cultural offering. It now boasts forty-seven museums across the Emirates. In Dubai, two museums tell the story of the Emirate's pre-unification history: Dubai Museum, which is housed in the oldest building in Dubai, the Al Fahidi Fort, and the newly opened Etihad Museum. There are also a plethora of small niche museums such as the coffee museum, the women's museum, and the camel museum. Dubai's "Museum of the Future," a first of its kind technological museum, is scheduled to open in 2019, and in Abu Dhabi, the Norman Foster-

designed Zayed National Museum which will
focus on local history is expected to open in the
next decade. The capital's Heritage Village is also a
good location to get a snapshot of the UAE's past.

The museums take a modern approach
to science that is somewhat at odds with the
worldview of the more conservative religious
thinkers, which makes an interesting contrast.
Most cultural attractions designate a day for
women and children only, charge low entrance
fees, and open reduced hours on Friday.

The "Desert Experience"

From any of the UAE's downtown hotels, you
can book a "desert safari," where dinner is served
and music is played in a traditional desert camp
setting. Some of these bear no resemblance to

Emirati heritage, with alcohol and international food served, and belly dancing (which comes from Egypt) offered as entertainment. Platinum Heritage Tours in Dubai offers more authentically Emirati pastimes such as falconry, camel riding, astronomy, and camel and lamb meat cooked *bedu*-style, in underground sand ovens.

Performance
Most Emirates have cultural foundations that put on re-creations of the past and its expression, often focusing on the spoken word accompanied by music or dance. But these aren't generally marketed to tourists. Qasr Al Sultan, a fort-like structure that opened in 2017 near the new Dubai Parks and Resorts theme parks, offers holidaymakers dazzlingly colorful dinner-shows that purport to tell the story of the UAE.

EATING OUT

Whatever type of food you prefer, however unusual, you can be sure to find it somewhere in the UAE. Restaurants include five-star hotel-based operations in the larger cities, which can be very expensive as tax and service charges of up to 20 percent are added onto the bills. Only in hotel facilities are customers served alcohol. Many restaurants offer free delivery, given that their premises may not be set up for conservative family dining. There are also restaurants providing low-cost cuisines to particular ethnic communities of migrant workers; these can be quite basic eateries where the customers are all men.

Coffee-shop Culture

All across the Middle East, men gather to discuss the day's events, politics, and life in general with their fellows. In the UAE, customarily the place they meet in is a *majlis,* or traditional coffeehouse. But nowadays it's just as likely to be the local Starbucks where electronic gadgets have replaced traditional games and discussion.

NIGHTCLUBS AND BARS

Nightclubs are tolerated in the UAE for the tax they generate. Many clubs attract cross-border visitors from Saudi Arabia, in addition

to international jetsetters who have made Dubai
one of the most fashionable places to visit. Illicit
appetites may also be satisfied, and overly friendly
ladies eager to strike up a conversation with men
at the bar are likely to expect payment for their
efforts.

SPORTS

Soccer is hugely popular with Emiratis, who follow
English, Italian, and Spanish football leagues with
great interest. The UAE also has its own domestic
league, which is keenly contested. The executives
of local teams are quite generous in salaries and
so can attract international stars such as Diego
Maradona, who manages Fujairah's team. The UAE
has also emerged as major financiers of soccer,
with Emirates Airlines sponsoring of Arsenal FC
and Paris Saint-Germain, and Abu Dhabi royals
investing heavily in Manchester City.

Sports bodies provide high-quality facilities and
large cash payments to entice leading international
stars to compete in the UAE in a variety of sports.

The Abu Dhabi Grand Prix, which is the last
race of the F1 season, is the biggest event on the
UAE's sporting calendar and draws in a variety
of high profile stars. Other sporting events
include Abu Dhabi Desert Challenge (off-road
motor racing), the Dubai Tennis Championships,
Abu Dhabi Golf Championship, and various
international cricket and rugby events.

Camel racing in the UAE is of course steeped in history, but it is also not without controversy. In 2005, the UAE government introduced strict new regulations aimed at protecting the camel jockeys after repeated allegations of child labor and human trafficking. Subsequently, more than a thousand young people formerly in the camel-racing world have been repatriated, mostly to South Asia. They have been replaced by robo-jockeys: mechanical devices perched on the backs of the camels that communicate between the camel owner and robo-jockeys by radio.

DISABILITY

Until recently, much stigma has been attached to those with special needs, leading families in the UAE to hide them away from the public eye. But the government has been keen to address this. Efforts have been made to make public spaces more accessible to those with physical disabilities, particularly in Dubai, and in 2019, Abu Dhabi is hosting the Special Olympics, a global competition for those with intellectual disabilities.

OUT OF TOWN

It is something of a cliché to observe that the desert is full of life, but you'd need the company of an expert to gain full appreciation of this fact.

Some visitors might enjoy moonlit picnics and
the romance of the night sky, which, away from
the bright city lights, can be exceptionally clear in
the desert and enable them to see shooting stars,
planets, and satellites normally impossible to
see. The best time of year to visit the desert is in
December, or January, after the annual rains, when
previously dormant, plants turn a lush green, and
small butterflies can be spotted flying between
them. Its easy to wonder whether the intricate
patterns of trails left behind of the dung beetles
on the sand dunes could have been the inspiration
behind the henna patterns that Emirati women still
proudly decorate themselves with today.

Wildlife

Birds are particularly plentiful in the skies over the
UAE, with perhaps the most striking being falcons,
buzzards, vultures, and owls. A good spot for

seeing them is in the gardens of the Mercure Hotel on the Jebel Hafeet, the Emirate's highest peak, in Al Ain. Parakeets, common mynah birds, and hoopoes are regular garden visitors, and close to the sea you can spot terns, ospreys, and flamingos. Goats wander the mountains of Fujairah and Ras al Khaimah, and foxes, and camels frequent the desert. The Al Wathba Wetland Reserve in Abu Dhabi is the best place to see the UAE's native plant life flourishing, as well as a host of migratory birds.

Dune-Bashing

One of the most popular forms of entertainment among adventurous souls is to chase up and down sand dunes in a four-by-four car. The dunes can be hair-raisingly steep. Many enjoy risking their vehicle against the force of gravity, to find out quite how acute an angle their cars can manage without toppling over into the sand.

chapter seven

TRAVEL, HEALTH, & SAFETY

ROADS AND TRAFFIC

The cheap price of oil and gas in the UAE has shaped a culture of car ownership. The high value that's placed on personal mobility is influenced by the remote desert origin of many tribes and the desire to have women protected from public view. Large, expensive four-by-four cars are favored, because they accommodate the larger families common in the Emirates, and they are practical for desert off-roading. Most Emirati families employ a live-in chauffer, because in the past, it was considered unseemly for Emirati women to drive. It's now becoming more prevalent for women to drive themselves, but large families still also rely on a driver to ferry multiple children about.

Most cars have tinted windows to shield passengers from the strong sunlight, and also to enhance privacy. A vehicle used to transport Emirati women is permitted to have darker tinted windows.

Although speed cameras and radar controls are now a common sight on the roads, there are still proportionately more road fatalities in the UAE than in other countries of a comparable level of development. To appreciate why, you have to understand that until the 1970s, it was more customary to travel by camel than by car. The first generation of Emirati drivers never took driving lessons, because there was no one to teach them, so good habits such as wearing seatbelts never become engrained. The UAE only made it mandatory to wear seat belts in 2017, but it is still usual to see children clambering about unrestrained.

The fast line in the UAE is jokingly referred to as the "Emirati Lane," as Emiratis tend to use it more than anyone else. Tailgating is a common tactic

deployed to encourage slower cars to move out of the way. Young Emirati males in particular have a penchant for speed, and while a reckless few take that urge onto the nation's roads, others channel it into dune-bashing (driving on the dunes), video games, go- karting, speedboating, or jet skiing.

It often appears as though people are in a hurry in the UAE, not necessarily to be punctual, but to arrive first, in order to assert their dominance. Some local people feel it is their right to cut in line, whether in supermarket queues or on the highways, reflecting the ever-present hierarchical nature of the society. It is never wise to try to confront such people in an angry manner.

Due to the transient nature of expatriate community, the second-hand car market is always booming. For those holding driving licenses from Western Europe, North America, other countries of the Gulf Cooperation Council (GCC), Australia, New Zealand, South Africa, and Turkey, applying for a UAE license is fairly straightforward, but other nationalities need to take a test.

As most drivers are foreign, each brings to the road different habits based on the driving culture of their respective countries. On the roads, Westerners tend to use the middle lanes, and the drivers of trucks and delivery vehicles, who are usually from Pakistan or Bangladesh, use the outer (slowest) lane, or specially designated truck roads whenever possible.

Emirati roads are modeled on the American system, with straight roads that run on a grid and almost always cross each other at traffic lights, as opposed to roundabouts. Wherever possible, long tunnels and spaghetti junctions have been built to ease the flow of traffic. Roads have as many as ten lanes on each side, so congestion is rare compared to most global cities. The exception is the Sharjah side of Dubai, where road blockages are common. Because the UAE's cities were designed to be car, rather than pedestrian friendly, walkers are often faced with crumbling sidewalks, steep curbs, and limited crossing points.

Visitors driving through the Emirates are likely to use the main E11 highway that runs parallel to the coast, all the way from Abu Dhabi to Ras Al Khaimah. This road encompasses the notorious "Sheikh Zayed Road" in Dubai, from where you can spot most of Dubai's landmark buildings along the way. There are no traffic lights and few easy stopping places en route, so drivers can find themselves longing for an opportunity to take a break and stretch their legs. Be warned that should you miss your turn, finding your way back to the right route can be an onerous task. Although there is always English signage, it can be confusing as roads often go by different names. As well as being known by their colloquial old name, roads in Abu Dhabi were recently renamed after members of the ruling family. To add to the confusion, roads in the UAE are also known by numbers, but somewhat exasperatingly, many numbered roads have recently been given new numbers. Add to this the problems that foreigners pronounce street names differently to Emiratis, and that there is no postcode system, it is no wonder that cab drivers can, at times, be bewildered.

Local Transportion

Although cab-hailing tech companies such as "Uber" have had difficulties getting past government regulations to become firmly established in the UAE, taxis tend to be reasonably priced, abundant, and reliable. In Dubai and Abu Dhabi, there is also the option of taking a water taxi to some touristy areas.

Dubai's metro system is reliable, clean, and a safe way to travel, as are the trams operating in Dubai's Jumeirah area. Elsewhere in the UAE, public transport is limited to a network of buses.

Intercity Travel

Coach and bus services link the major cities, comfortably and affordably, and minivans provide links with intercity services. Most stations are themselves comparatively well appointed, clean, and safe, as are nearly all the public spaces in the UAE. Front seats in buses are reserved for women and children and in some carriages on the subway and trams.

The UAE's railway line currently only exists to transport industrial products. The appetite for further public transport infrastructure is limited by the fact that Emiratis don't place a high value on public transport, because they rarely have reason to use it themselves.

Plans for a grand US $11 billion 745-mile (1,200 km) Etihad Rail network across the GCC, which, in the UAE, would span the country from

Saudi Arabia to Oman, have been stalled since oil prices began to slump in 2016, and an earlier plan for a subway system in Abu Dhabi also failed to gather momentum.

Instead, the focus has shifted to planning for new modes of transport: electric charging points are now generously dotted across the UAE's road network, and it is anticipated that 25 percent of Dubai's transportation will be autonomous by 2030. Crewless flying taxis are currently being tested.

The UAE has also positioned itself as an international hub for air travel. Dubai International Airport is currently in the world's top five busiest airports for international passenger traffic, and Abu Dhabi Airport, which currently has a capacity of 23 million passengers a year, is constructing a new midfield terminal that will accommodate an additional 30 million passengers per year, reflecting the anticipated increase in tourist numbers. Initially scheduled to open in 2017, the airport extension has also been a victim of the stagnating economy, and has been delayed until 2019.

WHERE TO STAY

The UAE boasts some of the most luxurious hotels in the world, and has garnered a reputation for extravagance and glamor. But, there are plenty of other options too for smaller budgets too.

Arabian Style

There are many upmarket "Arabian-themed" hotels in the UAE. They are often located far out in the desert with interiors inspired by *One Thousand and One Arabian Nights* and a skewed Western vision of Arabian opulence. Although beautiful, these hotels are not to be confused with the historical reality. Emirati forts were simple and sparsely furnished, and the palaces of some members of the UAE's royal family are filled with European antiques, rather than exuberant symbols of their Emirati heritage.

The best of these Arabian-themed hotels is the Tilal Liwa Hotel in Abu Dhabi's Rub al Khali desert. It truly seems to rise like a mirage from the sand dunes that surround it. From the pool, you can gaze through a sandstone archway out onto the dunes as you swim. Others offering comparable luxury are Qasr al Sarab, and in Dubai, the fortress-like Bab al Shams desert resort and spa.

For a more authentic desert retreat, the Arabian Nights Village in Abu Dhabi provides luxury-tented accommodations, palm houses, and a fort tower that echo the country's past, but with the added comforts of plush bathrooms and air conditioning.

Even UAE's many ultra-modern glass and steel hotels don't neglect traditional Arabian hospitality and offer guests Arabic coffee and dates as they check in.

Prime Locations

A central base to explore Dubai's heritage is the Arabian Courtyard Hotel & Spa, which is located opposite the Dubai Museum and a block away from Dubai's oldest neighborhood, the historic Al Fahidi Historical Neighborhood. You can also stay in a historic villa in one of Al Fahidi's winding pedestrian streets, at the boutique XVA Art Hotel.

Al Ain is the UAE's cultural heartland, with well-preserved, sandcastle-like forts and authentic traditional souks that have been preserved and recently opened up to the public. The city is a must for those wanting to understand what the UAE was like before the advent of oil wealth. The main city is served by leading hotel brands such as Hilton, and Rotana, and the local chain Danat that all provide five-star modern service with an Arabian touch.

Alternatively, Al Ain's Mercure Grand Hotel, which sits atop Jebel Hafeet Mountain at 3,000 feet (914 m), is a good choice for stargazers and those wanting to get away from the summer humidity. Anantara's Eastern Mangroves resort provides an ideal Arabian-themed base for kayaking along the waterways.

Futuristic Decadence

In Abu Dhabi, modern luxury is showcased at the Fairmont Bab Al Bahr Hotel and the Yas Viceroy Hotel that bridges over the Formula 1 racetrack at Yas Marina Circuit. Both hotels give the impression they were designed for the space age. At Jumeirah at Etihad you'll find wealthy Emiratis arriving in their Lamborghinis to sip coffee and enjoy the sea views from the sleek, polished lobby. Across the road is the golden Emirates Palace, literally dripping in gold, as its ceilings and walls

are decorated with gold leaf, and gold bars are available to buy from vending machines. But aside from all the bling on display, what makes this hotel stand out is its truly palatial beach club, which boasts a water park, cycling paths, and hammocks in the water, and is well worth a visit for those who can afford to splash out. For those who can't, you can visit the main wing of Emirates Palace for free, provided you are smartly and conservatively dressed, and are agreeable to buying a "camelchinno" (cappuccino made with camel milk) or other beverage from one of their food outlets. Emirates Palace also offers the opportunity to enjoy the sight of the new Al Nahyan royal palaces next door. They are an architectural triumph, reminiscent of the Taj Mahal, with striking gold leaf calligraphy adorning their rooftop domes.

In Dubai, those seeking ostentatious opulence will appreciate Burj Al Arab, the so-called "seven star" hotel in the shape of a *dhow* sail; it sits on its own island located off the coast of Jumeirah. This hotel is not only decked out in gold leaf, but also boasts a seafood restaurant, "Nathan Outlaw at Al Mahara," with floor-to-ceiling aquariums that make you feel as though you are dining in a glass submarine.

For fashionistas, the Palazzo Versace that overlooks Dubai Creek is the epitome of overstated Italian elegance, as Donatella Versace

herself took a hand in designing it, while the
Armani Hotel in the Burj Khalifa is somewhat
more understated and masculine in its design.

Longer-term Accommodations

The wealthier families looking to stay long-term
in the Emirates can afford to stay in palatial villas
in gated compounds, which might come with a
swimming pool and communal playgrounds, a

gym, and shops. But most expatriates settle with
lower-cost apartments, in buildings that usually
boast a rooftop pool and gym. These flats can
be spacious—the kind of accommodation that
is perhaps more familiar to Americans than
Europeans. Most apartments are let unfurnished,

devoid even of "white goods" such as fridges and freezers, and fittings such as curtain railings. Newcomers are usually issued with an allowance from their employer for furnishings. Ikea has outlets in Abu Dhabi and Dubai, and numerous community Facebook groups exist for expatriates to buy and sell second-hand furniture items. Residential compounds and apartment blocks usually have their own maintenance staff who can help out with fitting appliances.

HEALTH

The high standard of living experienced by most of Emiratis has meant that health across the society has improved. In 2016, life expectancy for Abu Dhabi Emiratis was 75.9 years for male citizens and 79.5 years for female citizens. The global average is 70 for men and 74 for women.

But Emiratis are starting to suffer from the problems brought about by affluence, including obesity that leads to heart disease and diabetes. Statistics show that more than half of all deaths in the country may be attributed to cardiovascular disease, road traffic accidents, cancer, and congenital abnormalities. Genetic blood abnormalities such as thalassemia are particularly prevalent, because of the high incidence of intermarriage within a comparatively small stock of people.

The UAE is investing in healthcare in the hope of attracting "medical tourists" from overseas, as well as catering to the needs of their own residents. Emiratis get free healthcare, which includes dental care, basic IVF, and mental health support, whereas the level of insured healthcare for expatriates is dependent upon their salary package.

The healthcare system is heavily commercialized, meaning that doctors are financially motivated to oversubscribe medications and give patients a range of medical tests that they might not always need. This has led to a growing number of Emiratis becoming addicted to prescription drugs, such as Tramadol, Xanax, and Valium.

Public hospitals provide care for all levels of medical insurance. Private hospitals, where standards of healthcare are thought to be higher, are selective. The increasing cost of healthcare means that insurance premiums are rising and the scope of ailments covered is being cut back. Maternity procedures, which used to be free for most expatriates, now increasingly come at a cost.

All migrants wishing to be employed in the UAE must be tested for the presence of HIV, and permission to remain is refused if the virus is found. Although Aids cases are low in the UAE, the Middle East is among the top two regions in the world with the fastest growing HIV epidemic.

SMOKING

Smoking is banned in public places such as shopping malls, but it is still legal to smoke in bars and restaurants. Smoking rates among Emirati men are still relatively high. According to City Hospital in Dubai 23 percent of men are smokers. Lung cancer is the most common form of cancer among them. But the sight of an Emirati female smoking in public would be sure to raise eyebrows among her compatriots.

Shisha, which is also known as hookah or "hubbly bubbly," is a tobacco smoked through a water pipe that's widely enjoyed throughout the Arab world.

Young Emirati males are particularly fond of smoking *dokha,* a combination of leaves, bark, and herbs, from a *medwakh* pipe. It's a heady blend that makes users immediately light-headed and bleary-eyed, and is believed to be very damaging to the health, although its exact contents are unknown. *Dokha* usage appears to be on the rise. The results of a 2016 health-screening program in Abu Dhabi showed that almost 30 percent of Emiratis in their thirties smoke from a *medwakh*. The government is keen to reduce smoking and introduced an excise duty in 2017 that doubled the price of tobacco. But the price of a packet of cigarettes is still much cheaper than in most Western countries.

SAFETY

One of the most attractive aspects of life in the UAE is that it feels safe. In fact, in a 2017 report prepared by the data firm Numbeo, Abu Dhabi was named the safest city in the world. There can be few other countries where you would find so many families out in the evenings enjoying the parks that are generally devoid of graffiti or vandalism. This may be, in part, because there are fewer young people living in the UAE who are of an age when they are most likely to get into skirmishes with the law. Expatriate families choose to move their youngsters home when they reach adolescence. Most of the UAE's universities are Emirati-only, so most expatriate young people will enrol in further education overseas.

The fear of being caught and the severe punishment that follows keeps acts of theft and violence at a comparatively low rate, as does the fact that no foreigners are permitted to live in the country if they do not have steady, gainful employment. However, in the corporate world, there is some temptation for people to defraud customers. Many people living in the UAE have at some point been called by a "company" giving them the good news that they have won a lottery, and then asking for their bank details in order to claim their prize.

Perhaps the most dangerous thing to do in the UAE is to drive during a heavy rainfall. The country's drainage was not designed to deal with heavy outbursts and as consequence flash floods are common. Fatal accidents are also common during foggy conditions, as drivers do not always keep to safe stopping distances or use the appropriate lights.

The police, who are mostly made up of Emiratis, have strict orders to uphold the law as it is given to them, and rarely show discretion. Be polite when dealing with them, and follow their instructions scrupulously. Police officers don't always have a firm grasp of English, and often police documents that you may be expected to sign, such as traffic violation notices, will be written only in Arabic. In such cases, try to find somebody who is able to translate before you sign anything.

The Threat of Terrorism
The UAE has firmly positioned itself as an ally of the developed Western nations, as well as Saudi Arabia. Together the seven Emirates are prepared to take steps to make sure that their security and reputation are not threatened by terrorist violence.

The UAE has thankfully not yet experienced a full-scale attack. ISIS is a Sunni militant group and it tends to attack Shia Muslims; the UAE is a Sunni society. But this does not mean that there have not been terror threats, and the UAE makes extensive use of surveillance and the secret police to combat these.

In 2015, an Islamist terror cell was foiled planning an attack against malls and hotels. The same year, an Emirati woman, motivated by extremist ideology, was executed for stabbing to death an American teacher, Ibolya Ryan. Perhaps the greatest threat to national security comes from the Houthis in Yemen who claim to have fired missiles (unsuccessfully) at targets in Abu Dhabi.

The danger is that in the wake of a wide-scale attack on the UAE, not only would its fledgling tourist industry be impacted, but also a proportion of its expatriate population would be prompted to move home, with potentially disastrous affects on the local economy.

BUSINESS BRIEFING

THE BUSINESS LANDSCAPE

Dubai International Financial Center (DIFC) is
the leading financial hub for the US $7.4 trillion
Middle East, Africa, and South Asia region. Abu
Dhabi is also tapping into emerging financial
markets through its own stock exchange at Abu
Dhabi Global Market, on Al Maryah Island. The
UAE is now at the forefront of the multibillion
dollar "global Islamic economy," leading the way
in the fields of modest fashion, halal media, and
halal cosmetics and pharmaceuticals. Sharjah is

the center of UAE's limited manufacturing base, as well having a successful tourist trade, drawing visitors from across the Arab world to its museum of Islamic civilization and well-preserved heritage area. The other Emirates are also increasingly garnering a reputation for tourism.

The UAE has been taking strides to wean itself off dependence on oil money, and is currently managing because it has succeeded in attracting some of the brightest minds in business, from both East and West. However, in its anxiety to appear futuristic and buoyant, the UAE has a tendency to gloss over any bad news, and a closer inspection reveals small cracks in their economic model, which in the future could present serious problems for the economy. Revenue from property rentals across the UAE has been on a downward spiral in recent years, with average residential rents in Abu Dhabi dropping by 11 percent year on year from 2017–2018, and this

trend shows no signs of abating. This reflects a slow exodus of foreign residents, not only because of job losses in the oil and gas sector, but also because significant cuts to expatriate salary packages have led many to return home. Government entities have cut back on their school allowances, for example, making it difficult for larger families to justify staying.

Dubai's economy is heavily dependent on the fact that the city is hosting Expo 2020, and significant investments have been made in infrastructure to accommodate the millions of guests the government anticipates will visit. But a question mark hangs over the post-Expo economy. Dubai's "if we build it, people will come" mentality has worked well for them so far, and the Emirate's trailblazing architecture has certainly ensured that "brand Dubai" has made itself known to the world. But its massive investment into gigantic new theme parks has so far had limited success. The triple-theme park complex of Dubai

Parks and Resorts, which promised to elevate Dubai to the status of the "Orlando of the Middle East," has so far failed to become a top attraction.

Nevertheless the UAE is still keenly developing its leisure industry. Abu Dhabi's Saadiyat Island, which means "Island of Happiness," is their US $ 27bn cultural district. It currently boasts a campus of New York University and the Louvre Abu Dhabi, a cultural collaboration with France, with more cultural institutions in the pipeline.

But the danger is that the UAE's own expatriate population will be priced out of being able to attend these prestigious new attractions.

The government has certainly succeeded in their efforts to make the UAE a peaceful, safe, and enjoyable place for people to live, and their hope is that expatriate residents will settle for a slimmed down pay package, because they prefer the quality of life in the UAE to that in their home country. And certainly, many will continue to stay in the UAE, because they appreciate the climate, the safety, and the values of the people, and because, in many cases, their own country is in turmoil.

THE LOCAL BUSINESS COMMUNITY

The UAE business community has identified its sustainable competitive advantages as being ownership of capital (they are cash rich) and ability to manage large-scale enterprises. Their lives contrast with those of the majority of the population, whose most common interactions with business are via food stores, supermarkets, private schools, and clinics. The UAE is essentially a dual economy, in which two separate systems coexist with each other, with people being dependent on members of the other sector but rarely coming into personal contact with them. But there is also a definite entrepreneurial section of society too, which is committed to creating and developing new business structures. Having capital behind them does help, but personal attributes are also proving important.

BUSINESS CULTURE

By law, businesses in the UAE (aside from those set up in designated Freezones) are required to be owned or operated in partnership with an Emirati businessperson. How business is conducted depends to a large extent on the local executive's international expertise, and whether they choose to be a silent or active business partner. Sometimes it is not easy to tell who the real boss is, as not all owners are interested in their businesses. But in some cases, they expect to be able to make all the important decisions and have appointed general managers so all relevant information can be brought to them for decisions to be made.

Many Emirati companies are run by family conglomerates with multiple business interests. While the company may initially have been set up some time ago by one man, whose name is still the public face of the company, it might be his son who is now managing it. Furthermore, because of the transient nature of expatriate society, there are times when continuity of a business project is impeded, because the most informed person has moved on.

If the people change, the business culture will also necessarily change. However, the physical spaces in which business deals take place tend to be similar to anywhere else in the world: large, spacious offices with excellent facilities.

BUSINESS ETHICS

Emiratis are as honest and hardworking as the people of any other country, but they are also subject to the same temptations. Deals involving large payments are not always made in a fully transparent way, so it is not surprising that sometimes people fail to adhere to the highest possible levels of behavior. However, since the country relies upon its reputation for honest dealing, serious efforts are spent to ensure that misappropriated funds are restored to their rightful owners. In Transparency International's international ethics rankings 2016, which compares countries to find those that are the least corrupt, the UAE had climbed to 24th place, level pegging with the Bahamas and Chile and markedly better than its neighbors Qatar (31st) and Saudi Arabia (62nd.)

Emirati laws that prevent freedom of association for trades unionists, and the lack of collective bargaining rights are considered by many to be unethical. During the country's last economic downturn, expatriate entrepreneurs who got into debt were summarily jailed for bankruptcy when checks bounced. In response to what many considered a disproportionately harsh practice, new bankruptcy laws were drafted in 2016 to remove the criminal offense of bankruptcy by default.

Companies in the UAE are nowadays expected to demonstrate their ethical commitment in terms of their impact on their stakeholders, society, and the environment. UAE firms are only beginning to come to grips with their environmental impact, and corporate social responsibility (CSR) is still a new phenomenon, but one that is quickly catching on. You can see CSR most evidently in action during Ramadan, when many businesses, particularly in Dubai, organize donations of food or toiletries for those in the labor camps, or some other charity initiative.

BUSINESS ETIQUETTE
It is advisable to have business cards ready to hand out when meeting new people, as they are still commonly used in the UAE. Remember to offer one with the right hand.

Handshakes are a common form of greeting in business, but in the UAE, the handshake is generally softer than in the West. Men should not shake hands with Emirati women unless the woman initiates it. And for Western women meeting Emirati men

for the first time, it is advisable to try to judge how
traditional you deem the man to be before offering
your hand. If he is likely to have been educated
in the West, he is unlikely to be embarrassed by a
businesswoman offering him her hand. A few words
of greeting in Arabic are also likely to be appreciated.

Expect to be offered coffee at the start of any
meeting, and accept at least one cup; taking more
than one sip is not necessary as cups are small. When
refusing another cup, gently waggle the cup between
thumb and forefinger to indicate you have had
enough. Wait calmly for the meeting to turn to the
issues you're interested in discussing, but be ready to
address them when the opportunity comes.

At conferences and large meetings, it is common
for a sheikh or someone of high standing to introduce
the proceedings. It is very important to sit politely
and quietly while they speak, with your phone on
silent, as a mark of respect. Status is essential to pay

heed to in business, so permit the senior person in any situation to take the leading role.

Many businesspeople maintain one or more technical advisors, who should be accorded respect. Advisors may come and go during meetings and this, like the answering of cell phones during an address, should not be construed as a lack of respect, but simply the way of doing things. Further, the moment at which a decision is actually made may not be entirely obvious. On some occasions, a consensus will emerge from discussions, at other times, eye contact between the decision-makers is sufficient to determine success or failure.

PRESENTATIONS

To conservative Emiratis, it is considered inappropriate to portray people in any way, and, in some cases, animals or anthropomorphic versions of inanimate objects can also cause offense. Indeed, any graphic or suggestion of Emirati men and women appearing together in the same physical space should be eliminated when presenting to a conservative Emirati audience.

NEGOTIATIONS

The way in which negotiations take place varies considerably, but in all cases, demonstrating loyalty and respect is critical. Traditional forms of negotiation depend upon finding common ties and affiliations as a means of assessing trustworthiness, after which the business details can be dealt with. Expect, therefore, for Emirati business partners to spend some time working out who is related to whom and what other connections exist. UAE business executives with international experience will get down to business more promptly, and follow a more Western negotiation style.

Many Emiratis are used to people coming to them with various business propositions, and therefore have no qualms in rejecting deals that do not appeal to them, or proposals that are not structured in ways they find attractive. They drive a hard bargain, and negotiations can become quite tough. A direct negative response can cause offense, so "no" should be framed in a polite manner. Agreements should only be considered final once all parties have parted ways.

CONTRACTS

Oral communication still carries more weight than the written word in the UAE. In traditional Emirati culture, a contract would not be necessary, since it is the underlying relationship between the people involved that provides the guarantee of compliance. Indeed, there may be occasions at which this old-fashioned approach to business may be carried out between people who trust each other sufficiently. However, the need for transparency has persuaded most UAE businesspeople of the value of adhering to contracts.

Contracts are created in line with standard international best practice, and once signed, all parties are expected to adhere to them according to UAE law. Documentation may be in Arabic, even when business partners speak good English, particularly in dealings with the government. In this case, establish a working relationship with a translation agency.

MEETINGS

Emiratis prefer to conduct business face to face. Indeed, it can seem that holding a meeting is an end in its own right and need not have any particular purpose other than getting people together. Initial introductory meetings, which are inevitably social in nature, must be held at the start of any new business venture so that people can get to know each other. In the past, this process could continue for some hours before any hint of business could be brought into play. These days, this process is speeded up, as there are now so many more business opportunities. Even so, the niceties of hospitality are still likely to be scrupulously observed.

Historically, when a person wished to meet an important figure, they would go to the appropriate tent and wait. The amount of time that would pass before the petitioner was admitted to see that person depended on the relative status of those involved. It would not be practical to operate such a system in the modern world, but some aspects of this practice do still linger. For example, there is the belief that everyone will get access to the leader if they are sufficiently persistent, and there is an obligation on the shoulders of leaders to be available to employees. One reason why Sheikh Zayed was so revered as a leader was that it was said his door was always open to his people. Foreign-born businesspeople should consider the implications of this, perhaps permitting access to all those who may wish to consult them on specific occasions.

Anticipate also that other people may come in and out of the meeting room on unrelated business. Don't address newly arriving people without being invited to do so by others, and avoid showing impatience. On the other hand, do set meeting objectives and focus on these as much as possible, no matter how sidetracked the discussion might become.

DEALING WITH THE GOVERNMENT

The UAE government has made considerable efforts to make it as easy as possible for people to deal with the state, largely by providing e-Government links and portals. However, accessing services and information in English in rural areas can still be problematic.

A number of business procedures tend to be organized quite differently in the UAE, and this can lead to disappointment. Government tenders, once a would-be contractor has passed the quality thresholds, are usually fiercely negotiated in terms of price. But it's not unusual for tender specifications then to be changed, and companies asked to re-present their bids accordingly.

Customer service at government service desks has improved over the years and generally, Emirati staff are professional and polite. However, the bureaucracy can be opaque and require more paperwork than seems necessary. Often, names, addresses, and other information have to be translated from English to Arabic or visa versa in order to process a form, and in doing so, it is easy for words to be misspelt or misconstrued.

WOMEN IN THE WORKPLACE

In recent years, the UAE government has devoted significant effort toward finding employment for its young women. Emirati women are now choosing to move into careers after completing their degrees, rather than rushing into marriage and children. Yet the fear that a daughter might become unmarriageable if she is too ambitious can still trouble even the most liberal of fathers. A 2015 GCC-wide study of women by the Pearl Initiative (a Gulf business-led organization promoting a corporate culture of accountability and transparency) found that although three quarters felt their families were supportive of their education and career, they were still hampered by traditional role models. Practical issues abound, but workplace environments are adapting so women need not be subject to close contact with male co-workers or customers. Separate rooms are provided for women to eat, drink, pray, and even nurse their babies. The government has stepped in to create jobs suitable for more conservative Emirati women, most commonly in the Department of Health or Education. Women need to work in a position in which they can remain living in their own home, since it still remains a taboo for women to live alone. Emirati women therefore often find it difficult to work unsociable hours, or undertake business trips that require overnighting away from home.

Organizations willing to take the necessary steps to accommodate local women often find their efforts are rewarded, as Emirati women are proving themselves to be ambitious, hard working, and enthusiastic, and as such are valuable assets to any company.

The business role of Muslim women from other countries working within the UAE differs little from that of men, although physical contact should still be avoided. Male visitors should develop the habit of being cautiously gentlemanly in crowds to avoid accidentally bumping into Muslim ladies. In shared elevators, he is advised to keep his eyes respectfully averted.

Western women in management positions should accustom themselves to the occasional unintended snub from male colleagues. Much of the business world is dominated by the rather macho oil exploration industry and by the preponderance of male migrant workers, who mostly hail from countries where women are still expected to stay at home. These employees may be less sympathetic to the concept of high-ranking career women. She may find that while male colleagues converse with jokey banter, they find it disconcerting if she tries to do the same. In the case of a young female college teacher conversing with her male students, it is best to earn respect by keeping the tone of conversation formal, and remembering that her students will be quite unused to chatting to unrelated members of the opposite sex.

Emiratization

Although expatriate workers are valued for their expertise, the government is keen to replace them with UAE nationals whenever it is possible to do so, under a process known as emiratization. There are worthy reasons for this: expatriates come and go, and some industries, such as the new nuclear energy sector, require employees dedicated to a long-term strategy. But the downside of emiratization is that it creates a culture of entitlement in which Emiratis expect to be given the top jobs, which they might not be qualified for.

When Emiratization is enforced, it can cause some resentment among foreign workers, who are expected to do the bulk of the work while their higher paid Emirati colleagues take more of a back-seat role. But this is not always the case. In some roles, such as the police force, for on top of their working duties, many Emirati employees have to take English classes in the evenings too. However, Emiratis are more inclined to seek employment with the government, who offer higher pay and better holiday allowances than private sector companies. When Emiratis do get involved in the private sector, it is usually as business partners rather than employees.

ECONOMIC FREE ZONES

The UAE government maintains a light hand on the economy, and it is usually not difficult for foreign investors to establish their businesses. Those who prefer to have a 100 percent ownership of their business, rather than working with an Emirati business partner, can opt for a license and office in one of forty-five designated free zones in the UAE, designed to encourage foreign investment with easier start-up processes and labor and immigration procedures. Each free zone has its own authority and rules. Dubai's twenty zones include Dubai Healthcare City (for medical start-ups), Dubai Studio City (a filmmaking hub), Dubai Internet City (for tech companies) and Dubai Media City (where CNN and other big news organizations have their Middle Eastern base.) It is hoped that by inviting foreign innovators into the UAE through these hubs it will stimulate a knowledge-based economy, which Dubai hopes will shape its future.

chapter nine

COMMUNICATING

THE COMMUNICATIONS REVOLUTION
The only two telecommunication providers in the
UAE— Etisalat and Du—are majority-owned by
government subsidiaries. This monopoly means
that broadband charges, TV conscription, and
cell phone services are comparatively expensive,
although both companies offer a reliable service in
return. It often surprises visitors that an Internet
connection is possible miles out into the desert.

Owing to cultural and to security concerns,
some international Web Sites are blocked, and
somewhat frustratingly for foreign visitors,
Skype and WhatsApp video services only work
intermittently. Sometimes these blockages are
for security reasons, or because the material a
site carries is judged to be obscene. Content of a
sexual nature is restricted but graphic violence
is usually tolerated. Occasionally, the blocking
removes access to other connected sites that
might be wholly inoffensive.

The online streaming company Netflix is
now popular, and people also watch TV shows

via a VPN network, although these are also sometimes blocked by the authorities.

Cinema outings are a popular pastime, but be warned that young audience members frequently chatter or play with their phones during the movie.

The strong taboos in place against unmarried men and women meeting up are being modified by the use of cell phones, since people can send messages to each other or use Bluetooth technology to initiate and sustain conversations at a chaste distance.

SOCIAL MEDIA

Alongside Qatar, the UAE has the highest social media penetration of any country in the world at 99 percent, according to a 2017 report by Hootsuite and We Are Social. Most Emiratis have at least two phones, one for communicating with family and one for work or friends. Many regard this social connectivity as both a blessing and a curse for Emirati society.

Photo and video sharing networks are hugely popular. According to a 2017 survey by the Federal Competitiveness and Statistics Authority, 96 percent of Emiratis use WhatsApp, 78 percent use Instagram, and 62 percent are on Snapchat. Facebook is more popular with expatriate residents.

Emirati girls enjoy posting their photographs online, but most are careful to ensure that certain pictures don't get into the wrong hands and compromise their reputation for modesty. Relationships before marriage are still taboo, and a single Emirati male (or his mother) will research any prospective Emirati bride on social media, to make sure she has been maintaining a wholesome reputation.

For some young men, social media is a way to explore illicit relationships. Some are experimenting with the dating app Tinder, which in the UAE is used by a significant number of prostitutes and other foreign women who see the financial value in having a relationship with a wealthy Gulf Arab man.

THE MEDIA

The UAE has become a magnet for filmmakers in recent years. Blockbuster franchises such as "Star Wars" and "Fast and Furious" have both been filmed in Abu Dhabi, and Dubai has been the location for "Star Trek Beyond," as well as several successful Bollywood movies. In an effort to cultivate a home-grown media industry, Abu Dhabi hosts film companies and app developers at the TwoFour54 media zone that overlooks the Sheikh Zayed Grand Mosque. The Dubai Film Festival shines the spotlight on hundreds of Arab-made films each year, as well as attracting international stars to its red carpet.

Abu Dhabi is also exploring TV opportunities: Sky News Arabia, launched in Abu Dhabi in 2012 and 50 percent owned by Abu Dhabi Media Investment Corporation, broadcasts across the Middle East and North Africa; and National Geographic Abu Dhabi, the official Arabic language edition of the National Geographic Channel, was launched in 2009.

The most reputable of the English newspapers is the Abu Dhabi-based broadsheet *The National* that was set up by former editors of the UK's *Telegraph* newspaper, and is a trusted source for local and regional news.

Like elsewhere, most people in the UAE now consume their news digitally through social media, which unfortunately means they are exposed to partisan content that merely echoes their own sentiments. Media laws forbid the press to report on anything that could damage the UAE's economy, meaning the perspective is inevitably rose-tinted in its outlook.

CONCLUSION

The Emirati culture of the UAE is intangible, remaining invisible to the vast majority of its visitors and expatriate community alike. To find it, you must be willing to look beyond the tourist enclaves, and try to form connections with the local people.

It is a country facing both the past and the future. There is a genuine and deep respect for the traditions and cultural practices of the past, even as society speeds into the future. The Emiratis embody this combination of past and present in a fascinating way, by understanding and accepting alternative forms of thinking, without wishing to change their own religious perspectives. With Expo 2020 on the horizon, the UAE continues its urban development at a pace not for the faint-hearted.

There has never been a more exciting time to visit the United Arab Emirates than now, when the country's young women are taking over positions of corporate and governmental power, and Dubai and Abu Dhabi are carving reputations as international business hubs.

Culturally it is making its mark with the opening of the Abu Dhabi Louvre Museum in 2017. Multibillion-dollar theme parks are part of the commitment to developing the area as a center for leisure.

The UAE's biggest export to the world is no longer oil, but hope, which it beams out to all its regional neighbors that are racked by war, unemployment, and political bickering. There is hope in the belief that the future technologies the UAE now embraces will provide solid foundations for a post-oil economy, and hope that cultures can coexist together—not necessarily on equal footing, but peacefully.

On the occasion of the International Women's Day, 2017, The Crown Prince of Abu Dhabi spoke of UAE's future:

"I am highly optimistic about the next fifty years, despite the fact that we live in a region facing various challenges and different viewpoints. However, I am confident that the UAE is just like a light in the dark. I am not exaggerating. I am citing figures, and figures do not lie. Regardless of the challenges it is facing, the UAE is a good model for the Middle East region. How many positive messages were sent from the Middle East to the rest of the world in the past sixty years? Well, your country sends a positive message to the world each and every day."

Further Reading

Al Fahim, Mohammed. *Rags to Riches: A Story of Abu Dhabi*.
Dubai: I.B. Tauris, 1998.
A revealing account of the changes that have occurred in Abu
Dhabi through the twentieth century through the eyes of a
boy who is now one of Abu Dhabi's most revered Emirati
businessman.

Gargash, Maha. *The Sand Fish: A Novel from Dubai*. New
York: Harper Perennial, 2009.
This novel, about a rebellious girl who is born into an Emirati
mountain tribe, brings to life, with historical accuracy, what it
was like to live in the UAE before the oil boom.

Heard-Bey, Frauke. *From Trucial States to United Arab
Emirates: A Society in Transition*. London and New York:
Longman, 1997.
This German author knows more about the history of the
UAE than almost anyone else alive today. She worked at Abu
Dhabi's Center for Documentation and Research, and still
lives in Abu Dhabi.

Henderson, Jocelyn. *The Gulf Wife, a Memoir*. Dubai:
Motivate Publishing, 2014.
A memoir of the wife of British diplomat Edward Henderson,
depicting how the UAE has changed through the decades.

Holton, Patricia. *Mother Without a Mask: A Westerner's Story
of her Close Relationship with a Royal Emirati Family*. London:
Kyle Cathie, 2004.
A semi-autobiographical account of a British woman's heart-
warming friendship with members of the Abu Dhabi royal
family through the decades.

Khateeb, Ahmed Mansour. *Sand Huts and Salty Water,
The Story of Abu Dhabi's First Schoolteacher*. Abu Dhabi:
MAKAREM LLC, 2016.

This is the autobiographical story of Abu Dhabi's first schoolteacher, and the colorful description of Abu Dhabi as a sleepy village he first arrived in back in 1958.

Morton, Quentin Michael. *Keepers of the Golden Shore A History of the United Arab Emirates*. London: Reaktion Books Ltd, 2016. One of the few comprehensive history books of the UAE.

Unnikrishnan, Deepak. *Temporary People*. Abu Dhabi: Restless Books, 2017.
A collection of surreal stories about the guest workers of the UAE.

Useful Web Sites

www.thenational.ae for news and commentary about the UAE

www.abudhabi.ae is the official government portal of Dubai government.

https://abudhabievents.ae to find out what festivals, concerts, sports events, and exhibitions are on in Abu Dhabi Emirate.

https://www.visitdubai.com/en/ for an A-Z of what visitors can enjoy in Dubai.

culture smart! uae

Index